## Intimacy Revealed

Cover design by Melinda VanLone at Book Cover Corner

ISBN -13: 978-0692335130 (HHH Books)

ISBN-10: 0692335137

Parker, J.

Intimacy Revealed / J. Parker — 1st ed.

*To four godly friends—C, J, L, and M—*
*who chat honestly with me about sex and marriage.*
*You encourage me to continue this ministry and*
*to nurture intimacy in my own marriage.*

# Intimacy Revealed

## 52 Devotions to Enhance Sex in Marriage

### J. Parker

HHH Books

# *About This Book*

I experienced a fundamental shift in my Christian journey when I finally realized the Gospel matters everywhere in my life.

The good news of Jesus' life, death, and resurrection has implications for how I live life in my community, in my workplace, in my church, in my home, and in my bedroom. The principles of love, grace, hope, and redemption extend even to the relationship and intimacy between husband and wife.

This book embraces that premise—that we should not compartmentalize our walk with the Lord by selecting only specific marriage scriptures to address marriage, but rather apply biblical principles we glean throughout His Word.

*Intimacy Revealed* will take you through Bible passages, some specific to marriage but many about our walk with God generally, and connect them to sexual intimacy with your husband. For each day, there is a scripture, thoughts to consider, questions to ask yourself, and a prayer.

Each devotion takes only a few minutes, and there are fifty-two devotions so you can study one each week. If it's difficult to carve out the same time each week, feel free to do a devotion on Tuesday of one week and Friday of the next. This is your devotional book, to use in the way that best fits your needs and your schedule.

While you may be tempted to deflect issues onto your spouse, these devotions are about working on yourself. It's a hard truth that you cannot change your spouse, but you can change yourself and exert a positive influence in your marriage. Take the challenge of being humble and looking at where God can work on you.

Of course, the scriptures in *Intimacy Revealed* have broader implications than the focus provided here. I encourage you to delve deeper into the Bible on your own. The Word of God is powerful, living, and active. And drawing closer to God, becoming more like Christ, and seeking His best for those around *you* will lead to greater wisdom and well-being for your marriage.

*May God bless you richly as you put His Word into practice in your marriage!*

Week 1

# Sex from the Beginning

*So the Lord God caused the man to fall into a deep sleep; and while he was sleeping, he took one of the man's ribs and then closed up the place with flesh. Then the Lord God made a woman from the rib he had taken out of the man, and he brought her to the man.*

*The man said,*

*"This is now bone of my bones*

*and flesh of my flesh;*

*she shall be called 'woman,'*

*for she was taken out of man."*

*That is why a man leaves his father and mother and is united to his wife, and they become one flesh.*

*Adam and his wife were both naked, and they felt no shame.*

— GENESIS 2:21-25

**U**nfortunately, some Christians have gotten the notion into their heads that physical desire and sexual acts came about as part of the sin that entered the world through Adam and Eve's disobedience. Yet this beautiful picture of marriage is told in Genesis 2. The Fall of Man occurs in the chapter following, not before. Indeed, in the previous chapter of Genesis, God instructs the first couple to *"be fruitful and increase in number"* (Genesis 1:28). God's design for sexual intimacy in marriage is shown even from the first chapter of the Bible. From the beginning, He intended married couples to become one flesh.

Our Heavenly Father's perfect plan was laid out in the Garden of Eden with a man and a woman shamelessly naked. I tend to think Adam was happily naked as well and grateful to his Creator for the view. Eve hadn't yet discovered fashion, but she was far more beautiful than any runway supermodel in her husband's eye. She was solely his, intended for companionship and partnership—*"bones of my bones and flesh of my flesh."*

When we make love in marriage, we express physically that deep connection. The first husband and wife, Adam and Eve, were intricately entwined, in that God created them from the same flesh (Adam's). In a sense, sex in marriage isn't just uniting in one flesh but also *reuniting*—returning to the intimacy God intended for husband and wife from the very beginning.

# ❧Questions❧

Do you see sexual intimacy as a gift from God? Has it felt more like a blessing or a curse? Why?

_____

_____

_____

_____

_____

What kind of "one flesh" experience do you desire to have in your marriage?

_____

_____

_____

_____

_____

## ❧*Prayer*❧

Lord, the sexual intimacy in my marriage is not everything it could be. Please help me to see Your plan as a gift to my marriage. Show me how to fully unite with my husband to become one flesh and to honor Your design. Give me an open heart and a hunger for Your words as I continue these devotions. In the name of Your Holy Son, Amen.

# More Than Physical

*Place me like a seal over your heart,*
*like a seal on your arm;*
*for love is as strong as death,*
*its jealousy unyielding as the grave.*

*It burns like blazing fire,*
*like a mighty flame.*
*Many waters cannot quench love;*
*rivers cannot sweep it away.*

*If one were to give*
*all the wealth of one's house for love,*
*it would be utterly scorned.*

— SONG OF SONGS 8:6-7

Song of Songs is the only book of the Bible dedicated to celebrating the sexual love between a husband and a wife. In this passage, the wife gives a clear picture of why their sexual love is so meaningful. Their intimacy comes from an unyielding love and commitment to one another: *"Like a seal over your heart."*

In Bible times, a seal guaranteed security or indicated ownership. Our marriage vows, lived out day-to-day, provide security and a sense of possession or belonging. *"My beloved is mine and I am his"* (Song of Songs 2:16, also 6:3). Sex within marriage isn't merely a physical act, but rather an expression of our unrelenting covenant of love.

Sex will feel more profound when we engage our hearts and our souls in this act with our husbands. When we recognize the vulnerability and intensity involved in interweaving our bodies for pleasure and togetherness. When we realize that God intended sex to be so much more than the physical. He intended it to deepen our seal-like love.

## ❧Questions❧

Does sex feel purely physical to you? What other forms of intimacy are involved (such as emotional, relational, recreational, spiritual)?

_____

_____

_____

_____

_____

How can you experience that deeper passion? How can you remind yourself during sex of its greater meaning and ability to connect you and your husband?

_____

_____

_____

_____

_____

## ❧ *Prayer* ❧

O Lord, I know that Your love for Your children is stronger than death. Because of Your profound love for us, You sacrificed Your own Son in the physical act of crucifixion. Sometimes You use the physical to reflect deeper meaning. Help me to see the deeper meaning of the physical act of sex with my husband. Help me to experience emotional and spiritual intimacy as we make love. Give us the strength and the courage to commit to an unyielding, burning, unquenchable lifetime of love. In the name of Your Precious Son, Amen.

## Delicately Woven

*For it was You who created my inward parts;*
*You knit me together in my mother's womb.*

*I will praise You*
*because I have been remarkably and wonderfully made.*

— Psalm 139:13-14

These days, "*I have been remarkably and wonderfully made*" sounds like something one might say after a series of plastic surgery procedures or a photo session with airbrushing and Photoshop treatment. As a wife, perhaps you feel that way only after the make-up is applied or flattering clothes hide flaws you're so intimately aware of. Maybe you felt wonderfully made once, when you were younger, but you struggle to see your beauty now.

Believe it, wife. God knit you together. He carefully crafted your body, from the tip of your busy head to the soles of your weary feet. When it comes to marital intimacy, He carefully wove the delicate parts only you and your husband see. And He didn't drop a single stitch.

Have you withheld allowing your husband to gaze on and delight in your body because you don't feel deep down that you're "*remarkably and wonderfully made*"? Let the world's unrealistic expectations and distorted ideals fall by the wayside. Shove aside the misgivings you have about your appearance. Believe what your husband and your Creator say about you: You are beautiful. *Remarkably and wonderfully made* by the Master.

# ❧Questions❧

Name three things you like about your body. From a facial feature to a body part to hair or skin color and beyond, what do you like about your current appearance?

_____

_____

_____

_____

_____

Have you ever withdrawn sexually from your husband due to a lack of confidence about your appearance? How would he desire you approach the marital bedroom?

_____

_____

_____

_____

## ❧*Prayer*❧

Perfect Creator, You knit me together in my mother's womb and Your gracious hand is on me still. You are the Master, which makes me Your masterpiece. Please help me to fully believe that I am remarkably and wonderfully made. Help me to pursue the health of this body You've given me, but to let go of unrealistic body ideals pushed by a secular world that doesn't understand the deeper meaning of sexual intimacy in marriage. Give me the confidence to offer my body to my husband so he can delight in my feminine beauty. In Jesus' name I pray, Amen.

# Looking to One
# Another's Interests

*Do nothing out of selfish ambition or vain conceit. Rather,*
*in humility value others above yourselves, not looking to your*
*own interests but each of you to the interests of the others.*

— PHILIPPIANS 2:3-4

Unfortunately, some spouses approach the marital bedroom with selfish ambition and vain conceit in their hearts. They view the marriage bed solely as a place to satisfy their desires and experience self-centered pleasure. Their spouse is not seen as the end, but as a means to an end—a way to achieve sexual gratification.

We should look to the sexual interests of our husband. We must let go of our selfishness and pursue what's best for both spouses. God wants us to enjoy ourselves, but also to bring enjoyment to our spouse.

In practice, that may mean adjusting your frequency to take into account both of your desires. It may involve asking your husband what touch feels good to him and following through with his requests. It may include engaging in new activities as you look for a win-win scenario for your marital intimacy. Pay attention to your own pleasure, of course, but look to your husband's interests as well.

# ❧*Questions*❧

In what way have you been selfish regarding the marriage bed?

_____

_____

_____

_____

_____

How can you pay better attention to his interests? What specific actions could make your marriage bed a place of fulfillment for both of you?

_____

_____

_____

_____

_____

## *Prayer*

Holy Father, You ask us to humble ourselves in so many ways and promise to bless us when we do. Help me to put my selfishness aside and to seek what's best for my husband and our marriage when it comes to sex. Guide me to express my own desires and to listen to my husband's desires. Give us unity in building sexual intimacy that strengthens our whole marriage. Let us always see one another as the end and not as a means to an end. In the name of Your Son, Amen.

# The Brokenhearted

*The Spirit of the Sovereign Lord is on me,
because the Lord has anointed me
to proclaim good news to the poor.*

*He has sent me to bind up the brokenhearted,
to proclaim freedom for the captives
and release from darkness for the prisoners,
to proclaim the year of the Lord's favor
and the day of vengeance of our God,
to comfort all who mourn,
and provide for those who grieve in Zion—
to bestow on them a crown of beauty
instead of ashes,
the oil of joy
instead of mourning,
and a garment of praise
instead of a spirit of despair.*

*They will be called oaks of righteousness,
a planting of the Lord
for the display of his splendor.*

— ISAIAH 61:1-3

S ome wives bear scars in the sexual arena. This is an area of special pain because it involves the most vulnerable parts of our bodies and our emotions. Perhaps you were molested, harshly punished for natural childhood curiosity, harassed, raped, verbally abused, cheated on, discarded. God sent His Son to "*bind up the brokenhearted,*" to "*comfort all who mourn,*" to turn your ashes to beauty, your mourning to joy, and your despair to praise.

God can heal any wound. Yes, it may take time, but He is there to do the binding, to hold you close in comfort, and to lift you up into better plans for your future. Know that whatever those painful memories of sexual mistreatment, that is not what God had in mind by providing marriage with sexual intimacy. The misuse of sex is like taking a bat, beating someone with it, and then saying, "See, this is a baseball bat." You would know what a bat is, but you wouldn't have any idea what it was really intended for.

Instead, believe in God's goodness and His desire to lovingly show you His better way. Let Him heal your pain, so you can see the blessing sex can be for your marriage now.

# ❧Questions❧

Have you been sexually mistreated in your past? How did that treatment affect your view of sex?

_____

_____

_____

_____

_____

Do you need to address past hurts—perhaps with the help of a friend, pastor, or counselor—to work through issues and find healing through your Heavenly Father? What steps have you taken or can you take toward healing?

_____

_____

_____

_____

_____

## ❧Prayer❧

Lord, You are our Healer, who cares for us when we have been injured. My view of sexuality has been tainted by past hurts, major or minor. But I want to bring my view of sexuality into line with Your design for intimacy in marriage. Please help me to work through the pain I've experienced, to heal from my wounds, and to experience the blessing of sex with my husband as You intended. Bind up my broken heart, turn my mourning to joy, and plant me like an oak of righteousness. In the name of the Great Physician Jesus, Amen.

# What Kind of Gift?

*Every good and perfect gift is from above,*
*coming down from the Father of the heavenly lights,*
*who does not change like shifting shadows.*

— JAMES 1:17

Is sex one of those good and perfect gifts? Do we see it that way? Whatever our Father of the heavenly lights creates is indeed good and perfect, and God created sex. It was His idea.

Unfortunately, we sometimes view this gift from God in a less than favorable way, because it's been tainted or distorted in some way. Satan wants to convince Christians to buy into the lie of sex as he presents it. That could mean viewing sex as a dirty or disgusting activity. It could mean reducing sex to a purely physical act. It could mean twisting sex into a series of more and more kinky acts, making the goal *how far can you push the envelope?*

Our challenge as Christians is to discover sex as that *"good and perfect gift...from above"*—to know what sexual intimacy looks like when it's passed from God's hands into the hands of husband and wife. We want to pursue the gift He intended sex in marriage to be, to recognize its beauty and its blessing. We want to appreciate that sex was God's idea and His children can revel in the intimacy it fosters in marriage.

# ❧*Questions*❧

Do you see sex as a *"good and perfect gift"*? Why or why not?

_____

_____

_____

_____

_____

_____

What changes would you like to make in how you view sex in your marriage?

_____

_____

_____

_____

_____

## ❧*Prayer*❧

O Father of heavenly lights, You shine Your blessings on us. Thank You for the good and perfect gift of sex for marriage. Help me to see Your gift as it is—a blessing for me, for my husband, and for our intimacy. Take any of my distorted thoughts and negative memories about sex and replace them with Your truth. Work in my husband's life as well to match his view of sex to Your design for marital intimacy. I pray the two of us will experience a thriving sex life that honors You in every way. To You and Your Son be all glory. In Jesus' name, Amen.

## Loving Deeply

*Above all, love each other deeply, because
love covers over a multitude of sins.*

— 1 PETER 4:8

**M**arriage researchers recently discovered what the Bible revealed in this verse almost 2,000 years ago: "Research suggests that what really separates the happy couples from the miserable is a healthy balance between their positive and negative interactions." And the "magic ratio" is 5 to 1[1]. That's five positive interactions required to counteract a single negative interaction in marriage.

Perhaps you don't need to track your good-bad ratio. Simply keep in mind the biblical prescription: Love deeply (five times?) to cover sin (one time?).

Couples who love each other deeply spend time together. They prioritize marriage. They nurture mutual friendship and shared faith. They attend to the small courtesies and the big gestures. They speak words of grace and encouragement. They invest in sexual connection and one another's pleasure.

Yes, even marital sex can help spouses look beyond one another's sins. It's difficult to stay angry with your husband when he selflessly took you to the pinnacle of pleasure. It's difficult for him to focus on your faults when you offer your body freely and fully in marital lovemaking. It's easier to concentrate on the good stuff of your marriage when you meld your bodies in passionate love.

Likewise, it's easier to have great sexual intimacy when you love each other deeply in other areas of your relationship. So love. Love deeply.

[1] Lisitsa, Ellie. "The Positive Perspective: Dr. Gottman's Magic Ratio!" The Gottman Relationship Blog. The Gottman Institute, 03 Dec. 2012. Web. 18 Jan. 2014.

# ❧Questions❧

Where do you struggle to love your husband deeply?

_____

_____

_____

_____

_____

What communicates deep love to your husband? What specific actions can you take to be more loving?

_____

_____

_____

_____

_____

## *Prayer*

You, O Lord, have shown us what deep love in action looks like. Help me to model Your perfect example of love in my attitudes, my words, and my actions toward my husband. Open my heart to those areas in which I've been unloving and help me to love him deeply. Thank You for covering over my multitude of sins with Your precious love. In Jesus' name, Amen.

## A Prayer for Unity

*My prayer is not for them alone. I pray also for those who will believe in me through their message, that all of them may be one, Father, just as you are in me and I am in you. May they also be in us so that the world may believe that you have sent me.*

— JOHN 17:20-21

**A**s Christians, we want to be united in the big stuff. In the message of Jesus Christ and His salvation for sinners. But sometimes our inner squabbles create cracks and gaps in that notion of being *one*.

In our Christian marriages, we want to be truly one with our husbands—united through the Father who blessed our union. But being divided in areas of our marriage, like sexuality, creates fault lines along the weak spots and threatens to sever our unity.

One of the biggest questions and challenges of sex in marriage is this: How can two distinct people, with their own histories and personalities and perspective, get on the same page when it comes to physical intimacy? What if one of you wants sex a lot, and the other, not so much? What if one of you wants to engage in a variety of practices, and the other is content with the tried-and-true? What if one of you desires more touch and affection as part of sexual intimacy, and the other is burning with desire to just get down to business?

God longs for us to be one, to be peacefully united and strengthened in our union with one another—in our friendships, our working relationships, our families, our marriage. Perhaps we simply need to begin with where Jesus began: praying for unity. We can pray that our marriages become as close as possible to the way the Father and Son are united. We can pray that our attitudes and decisions toward one another and the marriage bed are soaked with godliness and love. We can pray for God to bless us with wisdom and willingness to address those areas where we are divided and to resolve the discrepancies.

We can pray for our marital unity.

## ❧Questions❧

In what ways do you and your husband experience a lack of unity regarding sexual intimacy? Where do you desire to be better united?

_____

_____

_____

_____

_____

Do you regularly pray about the sexual relationship with your husband? How can you invite God to work in those cracks and gaps of division in your marriage?

_____

_____

_____

_____

_____

## ❧*Prayer*❧

Lord our Father, You long for Your children to be united, to be of one mind, just as You and Your Son are one. Place in me a longing to be united with my husband. Help us to see where we are divided in thought, in attitude, in action, and then to graciously address those gaps in our marriage. When it comes to sexual intimacy, open my mind and my heart to ways we can come together and find unity in our approach and our fulfillment. In the name of Your Son, Amen.

# Appreciating His Body

*My beloved is radiant and ruddy,*
*outstanding among ten thousand.*
*His head is purest gold;*
*his hair is wavy and black as a raven.*
*His eyes are like doves by the water streams,*
*washed in milk, mounted like jewels.*
*His cheeks are like beds of spice*
*yielding perfume.*
*His lips are like lilies dripping with myrrh.*
*His arms are rods of gold set with topaz.*
*His body is like polished ivory*
*decorated with lapis lazuli.*
*His legs are pillars of marble*
*set on bases of pure gold.*
*His appearance is like Lebanon,*
*choice as its cedars.*
*His mouth is sweetness itself;*
*he is altogether lovely.*
*This is my beloved, this is my friend,*
*daughters of Jerusalem.*

— PROVERBS 5:10-16

S ong of Songs, or Song of Solomon, is an intriguing
book—a celebration of marital love and intimacy
smack dab in the middle of the Bible. This eight-chap-
ter book is a collection of the declarations of love between a
husband and a wife. It includes three passages in which the
lovers describe in detail the beauty of their spouse's body.
This one is from the wife's point of view.

Why is this passage in our Holy Scriptures? Perhaps as an
example of how to appreciate our husband and the unique
form God gave him. There are several benefits to modeling
this approach and taking time to describe what physical features of your husband are handsome. First, it blesses your
husband to hear what you find attractive about his body.
Second, it fosters your own appreciation of his appeal. Third,
it honors God by showing your gratefulness for His handiwork. Fourth, it can increase your desire to engage physically
with your husband.

Notice that the wife doesn't simply say, "You're hot!"
(Although you can certainly say that too.) Rather, she con-
siders each feature and likens it to something valuable. Our
bodies are valuable—knit together by God Himself and
involved in the most intimate connection of husband and
wife. Treat your husband's body with love and appreciation.

# ❧*Questions*❧

List at least three physical features you enjoy about your husband body. Include at least one feature you only see when he's undressed.

_____

_____

_____

_____

_____

Have you expressed your appreciation for your husband's attractiveness to him lately? How can you make this a part of your marital intimacy?

_____

_____

_____

_____

_____

## ❧*Prayer*❧

Our Perfect Creator, You have made our bodies as expressions of Your glory and to honor You in our lives. Help me to delight in my husband's body, to note the beauty You have placed there, and to express how handsome he is to me. Please guide me to see him with Your eyes and to attend to the unique ways You have blessed him. Give me clear vision to see the male body as a beautiful form and to appreciate my husband's body in particular. In the name of our Lord Jesus, Amen.

# Braided Sexual Intimacy

*Two are better than one, because they have a good return
for their labor: If either of them falls down, one can
help the other up. But pity anyone who falls and has
no one to help them up. Also, if two lie down together,
they will keep warm. But how can one keep warm alone?
Though one may be overpowered, two can defend themselves.
A cord of three strands is not quickly broken.*

— ECCLESIASTES 4:9-12

**H**ow can one keep warm alone? There's something quite wonderful about sharing your bed with your husband. A bed is such an intimate place, a place you don't share with just anyone. Do you both feel welcomed and valued there? Is there a sense that this bed is shared, sacred, and supportive for both of you?

God's intent for our relationships is an interweaving of our lives. Whether in church friendships, in family relations, or in marriage, there is an emphasis on *we*. By sharing ourselves and our lives with another, we are stronger, better, more secure.

And the best situation is a cord of three strands—husband and wife interwoven with God Himself. In the marriage bed, two are indeed far better than one. But add a third—God Himself—and your marriage bed is blessed beyond measure. Not only is your body warmed, but your heart and soul too. And such a connection is not easily broken. It can better withstand the challenges of our lives.

# ❧Questions❧

What are some positives and negatives to sharing your bed with your husband? How can you make your bed a place of true warmth?

_____

_____

_____

_____

_____

Do you feel God's presence in your marriage bed? Is your marriage woven with God like a "cord of three strands"? How can you "braid" your sexual intimacy?

_____

_____

_____

_____

_____

## *Prayer*

Lord Father, You made us with a strong desire to connect to others—through friendships, family, and romantic love. I am stronger and better with the support of others in my life. Please help me to be a supportive force in my husband's life, including sexual intimacy. I invite You into our marriage bed to be the third strand we desperately need to remain strong and secure in our love. Give us not only the warmth of our bodies, but the warmth of Your love and blessing. In Jesus' name, Amen.

# Affair-Resistant Marriage

*Drink water from your own cistern,*
*running water from your own well.*

*Should your springs overflow in the streets,*
*your streams of water in the public squares?*

*Let them be yours alone,*
*never to be shared with strangers.*

*May your fountain be blessed,*
*and may you rejoice in the wife of your youth.*

*A loving doe, a graceful deer—*
*may her breasts satisfy you always,*
*may you ever be intoxicated with her love.*

— Proverbs 5:16-19

Proverbs 5 is often titled "Warning Against Adultery" or something similar. In this chapter, a father warns his son about the temptation of adultery. But this passage shows the biblical approach is more than that. It's more like a "Prescription for Faithfulness."

The wise father speaks candidly about the temptation of an adulterous woman, but he also speaks about the importance of fostering healthy sexuality in your own marriage. Not only is a husband (and a wife) to keep away from sexual temptation, but they should be "intoxicated" with love for their spouse.

Marriages can't be made affair-proof, but they can be affair-resistant. And one of the important ways to make that happen is to attend to the sexual relationship. Let your husband "drink from your cistern," rejoice in his wife, find satisfaction with your breasts, and be intoxicated. Willingly share your body with him sexually.

Not only is that okay with God, it's part of His prescription for faithfulness.

## ❧Questions❧

Have you withheld from your husband sexually? In what ways are you less engaged than you should be?

_____

_____

_____

_____

_____

Would your husband say his fountain is blessed, he is satisfied with your breasts, and he rejoices in his intimacy with you? Why or why not?

_____

_____

_____

_____

_____

# ❧*Prayer*❧

Wise and Loving Father, thank You for Your prescription for faithfulness. Help my husband and me to guard our eyes and our hearts against sexual temptation outside of marriage. Give me a clear understanding of how I can strengthen my sexual relationship with my husband, so we can remain faithful to one another and to Your Word. Help me to bless my husband and to satisfy his God-given sexual needs and desires. In the name of our faithful Savior, Jesus, Amen.

# Longing of a Higher-Drive Spouse

*Hope deferred makes the heart sick,*
*but a longing fulfilled is a tree of life.*

— PROVERBS 12:13

**W**hile much of Proverbs is instructive, some verses seem more observational. Like this one. It's an observed truth that when you hope for something and don't get it for a long time, your heart can feel sick. Just ask those who desperately need a job, yet remain unemployed; those who desire to be married, yet spend year after year single; or those who long for children, yet struggle with infertility.

Now consider the longing of a higher-desire spouse who is rejected over and over. Whether it's your husband or you, a marked imbalance in sex drives can result in a sick heart.

Oftentimes, a lower-desire spouse believes their rejection simply causes physical tension or hurt feelings. Instead, the rejected spouse likely aches far deeper, all the way down to their heart. Because, for them, making love both fosters and expresses love. Their hope is continually deferred, yet their longing doesn't cease.

But when our deepest desires are met—with a new career, a loving husband, a precious infant, sexual union with the spouse we love—that longing fulfilled is a tree of life. It bears fruit again and again.

## ❧*Questions*❧

Are you the higher- or lower-desire spouse? Has it always been that way, or has something changed in your level of desire or your husband's?

_____

_____

_____

_____

_____

How might frequent, intimate sex with your husband bear fruit for your marriage?

_____

_____

_____

_____

_____

## ❧*Prayer*❧

O Lord, You are the Author of hope and the fulfillment of our deepest longings. Please help me and my husband to look past our own desires and see clearly what the other is longing for in our marriage. Plant in us a desire to meet that longing. Bless our selfless actions with the reward of joy and a "tree of life" for our relationship. We give You all glory and honor, Father. In the name of Your Son, Amen.

## Focusing on Intimacy

*If a man has recently married, he must not be sent to war or have any other duty laid on him. For one year he is to be free to stay at home and bring happiness to the wife he has married.*

— DEUTERONOMY 24:5

**A**mong various rules and regulations given to the Israelites in the Book of Deuteronomy is this gem, which demonstrates yet again the importance God places on marriage. Even if the whole nation was at war, a newly married man was given a reprieve to work on building his covenant relationship with his bride. That first year would also involve exploring and establishing sexual intimacy.

Of course, no one can predict what challenges may come in the first year of a marriage. God's ideal is that we would spend our first year building a solid foundation, but maybe you didn't get that opportunity. Perhaps your first year of marriage was a struggle sexually. Perhaps you were faced with unexpected physical obstacles or the re-emergence of a painful history. Perhaps external circumstances—such as a family member's illness, work or military obligations, care of children—kept you both from devoting yourselves to learning about one another sexually.

But this verse in Deuteronomy shows God's heart on the matter: He wants us to take time to concentrate on our marital relationship—on getting to know one another more broadly, more deeply, more intimately. If you can take that first year of marriage and focus on one another, do so. But if you missed that window, it's not too late. Look at your obligations and your schedules and see what you can put aside to "*be free to stay home*" and then bring happiness to one another.

# ❧Questions❧

How was the first year of sexual intimacy in your marriage? Were you able to devote yourselves to getting to know one another emotionally, spiritually, and sexually? Why or why not? If you're still in your first year of marriage, how it is going thus far?

_____

_____

_____

_____

_____

Do you need to rebuild the foundation of your sexual intimacy? What can you do to return focus to that area of your marriage?

_____

_____

_____

_____

## ❧*Prayer*❧

Our Holy Father, You are the maker and sustainer of marriage. Thank You for this beautiful gift of companionship, support, and intimacy. Lord, You have placed a priority on marriage and commanded we give it time and attention. Please guide me to have the right focus on my husband and our covenant relationship. Strengthen our foundation of sexual intimacy, and help me to attend to the areas where we are weak. Give us an intense desire to bring happiness to one another—emotionally, spiritually, and sexually. In Jesus' name, Amen.

## Let No One Separate

*"Haven't you read," he replied, "that at the beginning the
Creator 'made them male and female,' and said, 'For this
reason a man will leave his father and mother and be
united to his wife, and the two will become one flesh'? S
o they are no longer two, but one flesh. Therefore what
God has joined together, let no one separate."*

— MATTHEW 19:4-6

Sometimes what separates us as a couple doesn't seem so much a "one," as in "*let no one separate.*" God joins a wife together with her husband, but family obligations, ministry activities, household to-dos, recreational desires, outside friendships, and more create separation in her marriage. Instead of prioritizing those intimate moments when husband and wife physically express their one-fleshness, life's other demands crowd out their sexual intimacy.

Yet these competing priorities could be attributed to a "one." Satan is a master of deception and division. If he cannot break up your marriage, he'll attempt to sap it of energy and intimacy. He'll attack us with busyness and laziness and complacency. He'll do what he can to separate husband and wife, even in the marital bedroom.

But what God has joined together, let no one—no one activity, no one to-do, no one ministry, and definitely not one prince of liars—separate. Cling to God's plan for sexual intimacy and let it strengthen your bond, the unique two-are-one covenant of marriage.

# ❧*Questions*❧

What separates you and your husband on a daily basis?

_____

_____

_____

_____

_____

What activities or obligations could you set aside, even for a season, to make more time for intimacy with your husband?

_____

_____

_____

_____

_____

## ❧*Prayer*❧

Almighty God, You have joined me to my husband and made us one flesh. You have intertwined our lives and our future, and I thank You for Your constant care. At times, I have taken this bond for granted, created separation between my husband and me. Please give me wisdom to recognize the attacks on my marriage—from Satan and from the world's daily demands. Help me to recognize even the good things in my life that keep me from my more important relationship and to focus on my marriage and becoming one flesh with my husband. I pray in the name of Jesus, Amen.

# Words Are Powerful

*Therefore encourage one another and build each other up, just as in fact you are doing.*

— 1 Thessalonians 5:11

**W**ords are powerful. Words have the ability to inform, persuade, discourage, uplift, and destroy. This instruction from Paul to *"encourage one another and build each other up"* is only one of many scriptures admonishing believers to take care with our words.

Yet sometimes, we take words for granted. We don't carefully consider the influence we have on our husbands in the words and tone we choose. Making love is a vulnerable encounter. You lay yourself bare, physically and emotionally, before your spouse and place your body and your pleasure in their hands. A harsh word or callous tone, or an outright insult, can cut off that connection like a kink in a water hose. When our words are gruff and insensitive, the marriage bed no longer feels like a place of security and intimacy.

But your words also possess the power to build up your husband and make him feel valued, potent, and loved. Compliment his body and his touch. Ensure him verbally of your desire and pleasure. Be gentle with requests and correction as he seeks to stimulate you better. Find the words to communicate he is a good lover. Encourage your husband throughout your marriage, including the way you speak about and to him in the bedroom.

# ❧*Questions*❧

What message have your words conveyed about sex with your husband?

_____

_____

_____

_____

_____

What words can you use to encourage your husband and build him up in your marriage bed? What honest and uplifting messages could you speak to him?

_____

_____

_____

_____

_____

## ❧*Prayer*❧

Lord, I confess my past sin of discouraging my husband with harsh words or withholding positive messages he needed to hear. Please give me the right words to speak, so I can communicate my love and desire for my husband. Help me to find ways to encourage him in the bedroom, to bless him with my words. In the name of our Lord and Savior, Amen.

# Our Perfect Husband

*And I will take you for my wife forever; I will take you for my wife in righteousness and in justice, in steadfast love, and in mercy. I will take you for my wife in faithfulness; and you shall know the Lord.*

— HOSEA 2:19-20

The Lord declares His intimate love by saying He will take us as His wife forever—in righteousness, in justice, in steadfast love, in mercy, in faithfulness. What an amazing portrait of our Perfect Husband!

God likens the marriage relationship to His relationship to us. The level of intimacy He desires with us is mirrored even in your sexual relationship with your husband. Indeed, the last sentence of the passage above is "*you shall know the Lord.*" The Hebrew word for know (*yada*) has several connotations, but it's the same word used in Genesis 4:1 (KJV): "*And Adam knew Eve his wife; and she conceived.*"

How well does your marriage paint a picture of covenant love? Does your sexual intimacy mirror the intimacy God desires to have with us? Do you approach the marital bed with the godly virtues of righteousness, justice, steadfast love, mercy, and faithfulness?

# ❧*Questions*❧

Why do you think God chose this analogy of husband and wife? How can our marriage help us better understand God, and His relationship with us help us better understand marriage?

_____

_____

_____

_____

_____

Where has your marriage bed fallen short of righteousness, justice, steadfast love, mercy, and faithfulness? Choose one virtue to focus on improving in your marital intimacy.

_____

_____

_____

_____

_____

## ❧*Prayer*❧

My God, You have proclaimed us to be Your bride and You to be our Perfect Husband. Thank You for Your tender care and steadfast love. I pray that my husband and I will mirror the intimacy You desire to have with us. Help us to see where we have strayed from the godly principles of righteousness, justice, love, mercy, and faithfulness, and to align ourselves with Your intentions for our marriage bed. Bless our sexual intimacy so that it reflects Your deep love for Your people. In Christ's name, Amen.

# Yielding to Sexual Intimacy

*The husband should fulfill his marital duty to his wife, and likewise the wife to her husband. The wife does not have authority over her own body but yields it to her husband. In the same way, the husband does not have authority over his own body but yields it to his wife. Do not deprive each other except perhaps by mutual consent and for a time, so that you may devote yourselves to prayer. Then come together again so that Satan will not tempt you because of your lack of self-control.*

— 1 Corinthians 7:3-5

This passage is often cited as a biblical command to have sex with your husband. Whenever he wants. But the tone of this passage actually describes the way a healthy, God-honoring marriage approaches sexuality.

Yes, a wife fulfills the obligation to connect physically and intimately with her husband, but he doesn't demand and she doesn't schlep to the bedroom with a must-do-it attitude. Rather, their marriage vows changed the way they viewed their own bodies—not merely as their own possession, which they certainly are, but also a blessing shared and yielded to their spouse.

It's a gift husband gives wife, and wife gives husband. One they mutually enjoy, yet can mutually forgo for a period of time to devote themselves to prayer.

Rather than focusing on sex as an obligation, consider the attitudes described here: understanding the importance of sex in marriage; yielding your body to your spouse; not avoiding the marriage bed and depriving your spouse of intimacy; mutually choosing when to engage sexually and when to pause to focus on spiritual endeavors. According to God's design, husband and wife are irrevocably interwoven—their bodies, their lives, their spirituality, their sexuality. As they should be.

# ❦Questions❦

Have you ever deprived your husband of the sexual intimacy God desires him to have in your marriage? Has your husband deprived you in some way?

_____

_____

_____

_____

How can you adjust your view of sexuality to align more closely with God's view of its significance in the marital relationship?

_____

_____

_____

_____

_____

## ❧*Prayer*❧

O Lord our Creator, You designed my body to connect sexually with my husband. Give me a full appreciation of that blessing and a willingness to yield myself to my husband for our mutual pleasure and connection. Search my thoughts and bring them into line with Your view of sexual intimacy in marriage. Help me to not deprive my husband of intimate connection with me, but rather to devote myself to mutually coming together so we both feel satisfied and cherished. In the name of Your Holy Son, Amen.

# The Flesh and the Spirit

*So I say, walk by the Spirit, and you will not gratify the desires of the flesh. For the flesh desires what is contrary to the Spirit, and the Spirit what is contrary to the flesh. They are in conflict with each other, so that you are not to do whatever you want. But if you are led by the Spirit, you are not under the law. The acts of the flesh are obvious: sexual immorality, impurity and debauchery; idolatry and witchcraft; hatred, discord, jealousy, fits of rage, selfish ambition, dissensions, factions and envy; drunkenness, orgies, and the like. I warn you, as I did before, that those who live like this will not inherit the kingdom of God. But the fruit of the Spirit is love, joy, peace, forbearance, kindness, goodness, faithfulness, gentleness and self-control. Against such things there is no law.*

— GALATIANS 5:16-23

So what is this distinction between flesh and spirit? All too often, Christians define sexuality as an act of the flesh. It's one of the reasons the Church has historically done a poor job of equipping marriages with a right view of God's gift of physical intimacy: We imagine this higher spirit self inside us, and then presume anything that involves our body is less than. Thus, sex becomes less noble, less godly, less appealing. After all, shouldn't Christians shun the things of the flesh?

But read that list again of what Paul defines as acts of the flesh. Marital intimacy isn't on there. When sex is mentioned, it's in the context of *sin* (sexual immorality, impurity, debauchery, orgies). When sex is removed from covenant love in marriage, stripped of its God-blessed state, it can become a thing of the flesh. Merely a selfish, physical act for the pleasure of those involved. Yet, the second list is just as illuminating—the list of the fruit of the Spirit.

Each of those virtues can be, and should be, present in the marriage relationship, including the marital bedroom. When we bring joy, peace, forbearance, kindness, goodness, faithfulness, gentleness, and self-control into the marriage bed, we honor our Lord and His special gift. There is no law against that. Such deep intimacy is not a thing of the flesh, but an awakening of God's spirit within us. When wrapped in the beautiful, God-given relationship of marriage, the act of sex can be a spirit-filled experience.

# ❧Questions❧

Have you struggled with viewing sex as a flesh-centered act? When does sex truly fall under the biblical definition of an act of the flesh?

_____

_____

_____

_____

_____

How can you live out the fruit of the Spirit in the marital bedroom?

_____

_____

_____

_____

_____

## ❧*Prayer*❧

Lord, the Church has often gotten it wrong when it comes to sex. Show us the ways we have misconstrued Your Word and open our eyes to the truth about physical intimacy. Give us wisdom to know when sexual activity is sinful and when it is God-honoring, and to preach accordingly. Help me to see sex as a blessing in my marriage and to bring the fruit of the Spirit into my marriage bed. Point out to me which virtues I lack when it comes to sexual intimacy with my husband and help me to grow in those areas. In the name of Your Son Jesus, Amen.

## Forgiving Wrongs

*Bear with each other and forgive whatever grievances you may have against one another. Forgive as the Lord forgave you.*

— COLOSSIANS 3:13

**T**his verse contains some high standards with the words *"whatever grievances"* and *"as the Lord forgave you."* Tall order, right? And how does it apply to the marital bedroom?

Most wives can think of a time when their husband didn't approach sexuality as he should. Perhaps he was selfish or demeaning in some way. Perhaps he ignored your sexual needs. Perhaps he withheld emotionally and spiritually from you. Perhaps he even has a stash of sexual sins from his past that have been hard to let go. Yet the command to forgive doesn't stop at the bedroom door.

Rather, we are instructed to give the benefit of the doubt, to extend understanding and grace, to forgive as the Lord forgave us. Is that always easy? No. But we have God's guidance and wisdom when we ask for it. We can pursue better, healthier sexuality in our marriage, while finding a way to forgive the grievances we have grasped in our hearts for too long.

# ❧*Questions*❧

Has your husband wronged you in some way regarding sexual intimacy? How have you felt wounded?

_____

_____

_____

_____

_____

Have you wounded your husband in some way? Have you sought forgiveness from him for your own offenses?

_____

_____

_____

_____

_____

## ❧*Prayer*❧

Lord Jehovah, You have forgiven us so much and continue to wash us clean as we come before You to confess and repent of our wrongdoings. Holy Father, help my husband and I to confess how we have wounded each other, to align ourselves with Your design for our sexual intimacy, and to forgive each other—as you, o Lord, have forgiven us. Let Your forgiveness flow through me to him, washing our relationship clean of past sins so that we can be renewed. In the name of Your Son, Amen.

# Sex and Our Relationship with Christ

*"For this reason a man will leave his father and mother and be united to his wife, and the two will become one flesh." This is a profound mystery—but I am talking about Christ and the church. However, each one of you also must love his wife as he loves himself, and the wife must respect her husband.*

— EPHESIANS 5:31-33

**H**ave you truly considered this analogy the apostle Paul makes? When you make love with your husband, you reflect something mysterious and true about our relationship to Christ. Experiencing godly sex in marriage can help us understand the deep intimacy Jesus Himself desires to have with His followers.

What qualities of healthy marital sex reflect this intimacy we can have with our Savior?

When we experience God-honoring sex with our husband, we are focused on him—committed, trusting, connected, excited, and fulfilled. When we have a loving relationship with Christ, we are focused on him—committed, trusting, connected, excited, and fulfilled. In both, we get caught up in the beautiful sensation and profound certainty that we are securely united with our bridegroom.

Just as becoming a parent often increases a believer's understanding of God as Father, experiencing healthy sexual intimacy in marriage can illuminate deep truths about how Christ relates to His people. Godly marital sex is worth pursuing for its own sake, and for what it reveals about our walk with Jesus Christ. Revel in the beauty of marital intimacy, and recognize it as a peek into the intimacy Christ desires with us.

# ❧*Questions*❧

How does the one-flesh bonding of marital sex resemble or reflect our union with Jesus Christ as believers?

_____

_____

_____

_____

_____

Does sex in your marriage feel intimately bonding? Is there love and respect in your marriage bed? How can you nurture it?

_____

_____

_____

_____

_____

## ❧*Prayer*❧

Lord Father, thank You for providing a bridegroom for Your Church—Jesus Christ. Help me to experience deeper intimacy with my husband in the marriage bed and to apply that understanding to my relationship with Christ. Show me the areas in which I'm holding my body and my heart back from my husband, and help me to give myself more freely and fully. Draw me closer to my husband and to my Lord. In the name of my beautiful Savior, Amen.

# Sins of the Past

*Or do you not know that wrongdoers will not inherit the kingdom of God? Do not be deceived: Neither the sexually immoral nor idolaters nor adulterers nor men who have sex with men nor thieves nor the greedy nor drunkards nor slanderers nor swindlers will inherit the kingdom of God. And that is what some of you were. But you were washed, you were sanctified, you were justified in the name of the Lord Jesus Christ and by the Spirit of our God.*

— 1 Corinthians 6:9-11

A mong the nine sins listed here, three of them are sexual in nature. Clearly, God is concerned about His people preserving the gift of sexuality in its right context of marital intimacy. If sinners continue in sexual sin, they are denied the opportunity to live as an heir in God's kingdom. However, this passage doesn't dwell on the negative consequence of sin. Instead, we have the grace of our Lord, Jesus Christ.

Perhaps you or your husband has sexual sin in your past. That sin left traces of guilt and shame, making it even more difficult to engage fully and freely in marital sex. But *"you were washed, you were sanctified, you were justified."* Sexual sin doesn't keep its hold on you and your marriage any longer. Christ Jesus took care of that sin, and as heirs of God's kingdom, we can and should enjoy all the gifts from the Father. One of those gifts is healthy sexuality in your marriage.

It may take time to build the physical intimacy you and your husband desire, but your first step could be believing these past sexual sins do not hinder God's full blessing in marriage. You were *washed, sanctified, justified*—meaning that was then, this is now. You have a fresh start and an opportunity to live into the blessings of satisfying intimacy in your marriage. Believe it. Know it. Live it.

# ❧ Questions ❧

Have you or your husband committed sexual sin? In what way has your relationship felt the negative consequences of those decisions?

_____

_____

_____

_____

_____

Have you or your husband confessed and repented of that sin? What still troubles you about that sexual sin? And how can you let go of that guilt and shame and lean into the blessing of God's intimacy in your marriage?

_____

_____

_____

_____

_____

## ❧*Prayer*❧

Our Father of comfort, You know our deepest struggles and our past sins. I confess my failings to you, knowing I haven't always pursued Your higher plans for purity and intimacy. Thank You for Your forgiveness and for washing, sanctifying, and justifying me. Help me to fully believe that my sins, and those of my husband, can be washed away completely and You will bless us in our marriage. Give me Your eyes to see the purity we now have before You because of Christ. It's in His name I pray, Amen.

Week 22

# Attending to His Body

*"Now that I, your Lord and Teacher, have washed your feet, you also should wash one another's feet. I have set you an example that you should do as I have done for you."*

— JOHN 13:14-15

Jesus instructed His disciples to serve one another. But rather than simply give the command, He showed what true service looks like. He knelt before them like a lowly servant, held the weary and dusty feet of His close friends, and took care to wash and dry until their feet were fresh and clean.

Imagine bringing that same attitude toward your husband into the marital bedroom. Do you give your husband's body the same careful attention Jesus gave to His disciples' feet? How could bring that lingering touch and attention into your close times together? Could you wash his body for him in the shower or the bathtub? Could you apply lotion to his dry skin or massage his weary muscles? Could you rub his feet or run your hands through his hair and scalp? How can you serve him with the attitude of Jesus?

Follow the example of Jesus caring for something as seemingly insignificant as feet—showing how significant these kindnesses truly are. Linger with your hands on your husband and focus your heart on serving him.

# ❧*Questions*❧

Have you shown the kind of careful attention to your husband's body that Jesus showed to His disciples feet? Why or why not?

_____

_____

_____

_____

_____

What tender activities of touch and care might your husband enjoy? When can you plan to show him special kindness in this way?

_____

_____

_____

_____

_____

## ❧Prayer❧

Dear Lord, You gave such careful attention to the creation of our bodies—giving each part an important role in the whole. Help me to appreciate my husband's body for the wonder it is and as a temple of Your Spirit. Show me how to serve my husband through gentle care and touch. Give me the attitude of Your Son Jesus, in whose name I pray. Amen.

# Not Withholding Good

*Do not withhold good from those to whom it is due,*
*when it is in your power to act.*

*Do not say to your neighbor,*
*"Come back tomorrow and I'll give it to you"—*
*when you already have it with you.*

— Proverbs 3:27-28

This proverb says you shouldn't withhold from someone what he is due when it's in your power to give it. Yet sometimes, wives withhold from their husbands the sexual intimacy they are due. Yes, sometimes you don't *have it with you*—such as when you are feeling unwell or family urgencies demand your attention. There are times when it's okay to say "not now, but later."

But what about saying no when you simply don't feel like it? It is in your power to be sexually intimate with your husband, even if your drive isn't present at the very moment he suggests it. What about holding back from fully participating in the experience? The Bible is clear that your husband is due a willing sexual partner. If you've been withholding, how can you change that around? How can you apply this proverb to your marriage bed?

And if you're the higher drive spouse, and your husband has withheld from you, you are understandably hurt. You are due sexual intimacy in marriage, but you can only change yourself. So consider what he's due in helping him with his lack of desire: Give him patience, understanding, communication, and commitment to work through the issues and develop a stronger, healthier sex life together.

# ❧Questions❧

Has one of you withheld sexual intimacy the other spouse is due? What toll has that taken on your marriage?

_____

_____

_____

_____

_____

How can you nurture the sense that you "*have it with you*" so you can fully engage sexually with your husband?

_____

_____

_____

_____

_____

## ❧*Prayer*❧

Lord, I understand biblical principles can be applied to all areas of my life. Please help me to see how living out these higher ideals can positively affect my marriage bed. Show me where I have withheld myself from my husband and what he is due from his wife. Give me an inner will and a loving heart to fully foster the sexual intimacy in my marriage. In the holy name of Jesus, Amen.

# Better Love in the Bedroom

*Love is patient, love is kind. It does not envy, it does not boast, it is not proud. It does not dishonor others, it is not self-seeking, it is not easily angered, it keeps no record of wrongs. Love does not delight in evil but rejoices with the truth. It always protects, always trusts, always hopes, always perseveres.*

— 1 CORINTHIANS 13:4-6

**B**y God's design, sex in marriage is an expression and nurturer of love between husband and wife. So when we read the passage about love from 1 Corinthians 13, do we consider that it all applies to the marital bedroom? Whatever is loving outside the marriage bed is loving in the marriage bed as well.

What would sexual intimacy look like if you and your husband were always patient and kind? Would you take more time to explore one another's pleasure, to discuss and resolve challenges, to touch and embrace more fully?

If you were never boastful or proud? Would you reconsider the usual stance that your own thoughts on sexuality must be the right ones? Would you listen more openly to your husband's perspective on sex and try to understand where he's coming from?

If your sexual love wasn't self-seeking, how could you turn your attention more to your husband?

If it was not easily angered and kept no record of wrongs, what past infractions and current resentment would you let go?

If it didn't delight in evil but rejoiced in the truth, what sexual lies would you need to discard? What wrong attitudes and acts has Satan used to divide you in your marriage, and what truths does God teach regarding sex?

And finally, if sexual love always protects, always trusts, always hopes, always perseveres, what would that look like in your marital bedroom? What could you do to protect the sacred marriage bed? To trust your husband? To hope that, whatever your marital intimacy is now, it can improve and honor God? Despite prior misunderstandings and current challenges, how can you persevere in fostering the best sexual intimacy you can experience in your marriage?

Wrap your marriage bed in 1 Corinthians 13 love, and your sexual intimacy will be blessed.

# ❧Questions❧

Reading back through the passage, which loving trait is most difficult for you to apply to the marriage bed? Why is that trait so difficult to extend to your husband when it comes to sex?

_____

_____

_____

_____

Choose one trait you want to develop more. What specific steps or actions can you take to develop that trait for yourself and for your marital intimacy?

_____

_____

_____

_____

# *Prayer*

Father, Your love is higher than the heavens and unfailing to Your children. I pray Your love will flow through me toward my husband, blessing him in every way possible. Show me where I've withheld love from him in our marriage bed. Help me to put into action the love described in 1 Corinthians 13 in our marriage, including our physical intimacy. Wrap our marriage bed in Your love, Your truth, Your protection, and Your hope. In the name of Your loving Son, Amen.

# No Place for Deceit

*Do not lie to each other, since you have taken off your old
self with its practices and have put on the new self, which is
being renewed in knowledge in the image of its Creator.*

— Colossians 3:9-10

This simple command, *"Do not lie to each other,"* has implications even for the marriage bed.

Your bedroom is no place for deceit. The marriage bed should be a place of security and trust. That means you shouldn't perpetuate lies to your husband, even small deceptions. Instead, you should deal honestly with whatever you experience and whatever challenges you.

If you're not having an orgasm, don't fake it. If you're struggling with libido or figuring out what feels good, let him in on the deal. If you wish he'd do something different, don't answer that he nailed it perfectly. Don't pretend everything is fine if it's not.

Be gentle, but be honest. In the image of our Creator, deal honestly with your husband. Then seek authentic ways to experience pleasure and nurture intimacy together.

## ❧Questions❧

Have you lied to your husband about your past, your desires, or your pleasure? Do you need to come clean about any deceptions regarding your marriage bed?

_____

_____

_____

_____

_____

Being honest doesn't mean you share every detail of your past or your exact thoughts, but you don't lie or deceive your husband. What truths do you really need to share, and how can you share them gently and lovingly with him?

_____

_____

_____

_____

_____

## ❧Prayer❧

Dear God, You are the author of all truth. Please reveal to me the ways I've deceived my husband regarding our marriage bed. Give me courage to confess my lies and commit to being honest. Help us to deal honestly, openly, and lovingly with the truth. I pray that our marital bedroom will always be a place of security and trust. In the name of Your Holy Son, Amen.

# Answering Sexual Temptation

*Flee from sexual immorality. All other sins a person commits are outside the body, but whoever sins sexually, sins against their own body. Do you not know that your bodies are temples of the Holy Spirit, who is in you, whom you have received from God? You are not your own; you were bought at a price. Therefore honor God with your bodies.*

— 1 Corinthians 6:18-20

**W**hen temptation comes our way, we turn to the tried-and-true biblical tactics of prayer, citation of scripture, and consulting Christian advisers. But when it comes to sexual temptation, the overriding message of the Bible is not pray, fight, or consult...but flee. That's right: *Flee.* Run like the wind, get outta Dodge, go far, far away. Avoid it like it's a poisonous viper waiting to strike.

That was Joseph's response when faced with sexual temptation from Potiphar's wife—to bolt from the house as quickly as possible (Genesis 39). Proverbs 5:7 warns the same with its instruction to "*keep to a path far from [the adulterous woman], do not go near the door of her house.*" Our defense against getting entangled in physical or emotional affairs is to stay away from whatever might draw us in, so we can remain true to our marriage and honor God with our bodies.

Temptation these days comes in different forms than in Bible times. Perhaps it's the friend request from an old flame on a social media site, or an invitation to lunch with a male co-worker, or even the lure of spending extra time with a fellow ministry volunteer. We can think that we have it all under control, that we are sufficiently armed with scripture and prayer, that we are stronger than the temptation. God will hold You in His capable hands, but He also encourages you to be realistic and be smart. If necessary, follow His command to simply *flee.*

# ❧Questions❧

During the time you've been married, have you ever been sexually tempted? Do you believe you could be tempted in the future?

_____

_____

_____

_____

_____

What would it look like to flee sexual temptation? What boundaries or strategies could you use if needed?

_____

_____

_____

_____

_____

## ❧*Prayer*❧

Lord, when I call out to You, You answer. You know the desires and weaknesses of my heart. I long to be loyal to Your Word and to my marriage. May I faithfully soak up scriptures to arm myself in advance and continue to ask for strength from You. Yet if I'm faced with sexual temptation, help me to follow Your command to simply flee. Set my feet in a direction away from sin and guide me to safety. Redirect my eyes and my heart to my husband and our marriage bed. In the name of Jesus, Amen.

## An Honored and Pure Marriage Bed

*Marriage should be honored by all, and the marriage bed kept pure, for God will judge the adulterer and all the sexually immoral.*

— HEBREWS 13:4

The Bible is extremely clear: Adultery, bad. Sexual purity, good. If you get nothing else from Scripture about sexuality, that's indisputable. So does this mean merely that a spouse shouldn't sleep with someone besides his or her mate? That's a baseline, but it's not the only thing meant by honored and pure.

Third parties of any kind meet the Bible's definition of adultery. Jesus said that lusting after someone besides your spouse is adulterous (Matthew 5:27-30). Considering this, how is it honoring your marriage bed to imagine and lust after the hero from the romance novel you just read? Or the man candy in a magazine or Internet photo you saw earlier today? Or to recall a past lover from your premarital days? Perhaps this isn't your struggle, but it is a common one. We are a surrounded by sexual images and fantasies, and those can easily implant themselves into our brain and become mental scripts we play in our heads.

Healthy marital sex is focused on the interaction between husband and wife, and we must drive out anything that competes for that special moment with our husband. Honor involves paying attention, being engaged, focusing on the item we honor—the marriage bed. Third parties and stray thoughts keep us from giving our marriage bed its due. Keep the marriage bed pure: certainly pure from adultery and also pure from distraction.

## ❧Questions❧

What do you think it means to keep the marriage bed honored and pure?

_____

_____

_____

_____

_____

What do you struggle with in your marriage bed—third parties in your mind or lack of focus on your husband? How can you address problems in this area?

_____

_____

_____

_____

_____

# ❧*Prayer*❧

My Lord, my Father, what a blessing my marriage bed is to me and to my husband! Thank You for the reminders throughout Your Word that sex is to be shared only between husband and wife and has special meaning in marriage. Guide my mind to concentrate only on my husband when we make love. Take away any thoughts of others or distractions that would pull my focus away from him. Help me to convey to my husband that I honor our sexual intimacy and want it to remain pure in every way. In Jesus' holy name, Amen.

# Faithfulness

*Another thing you do: You flood the Lord's altar with tears. You weep and wail because he no longer looks with favor on your offerings or accepts them with pleasure from your hands. You ask, "Why?" It is because the Lord is the witness between you and the wife of your youth. You have been unfaithful to her, though she is your partner, the wife of your marriage covenant.*

— MALACHI 2:13-14

The Bible teaches that one spouse's continual mistreatment of the other hinders their relationship to God. These obstacles are not merely pebbles over which to stumble, but boulders that make it hard for us to see God and for God to see us. God isn't all that inclined to pay attention to acts of worship that are trampled on by disloyalty in our relationships.

Thus, faithfulness in marriage matters. And being faithful includes being appropriately sexual with your spouse. It's part of the marriage covenant.

We may try to compartmentalize our sexuality or our marriage apart from our spirituality. But God sees us as a whole person—considering both our obedience and our rebellion across the board. We can't expect to go to church, sing happy hymns, pray now and then, and "get away with it." The Lord is our witness. He sees how we conduct ourselves, and He wants to draw you into an intimate relationship with Him and a right relationship to your husband. Consider how your marital intimacy is keeping that covenant or hindering your intimacy with God.

## ❧Questions❧

What do you think it means that "*the Lord is the witness*"? How does He keep watch over our marriages?

_____

_____

_____

_____

_____

How does a good marriage and an intimate sexual relationship with your husband serve your spiritual life? What benefits to your walk with God might there be in faithfulness to the marriage bed?

_____

_____

_____

_____

_____

### ❧*Prayer*❧

Lord, may Your ears always be open to my prayers. May my words and actions honor You and keep Your ears attentive to my praise and my pleas. Teach me what it is to be faithful to my husband in every area of our marriage, including sexual intimacy. Help me to keep the covenant we have made. Let my ears always be open to You, as I pray that Your ears are open to me. In the name of Your Holy Son, Amen.

# Doing Good

*Therefore, as we have opportunity, let us do good to all people, especially to those who belong to the family of believers.*

— GALATIANS 6:10

**D**oing good comes in many forms. It can be the care of a mother who helps her child with homework or tucks him into bed at night with a prayer on her lips. It can be the delivery of food to a needy family or visiting a friend in the hospital. It can be the words of encouragement to a struggling fellow Christian or a faith seeker. It can be the simple courtesy of letting another driver merge in front of you in heavy traffic. It can even be the generosity of meeting your husband's sexual need and desire for physical intimacy with his wife.

It's easy to put other good acts ahead of our sexual intimacy in marriage, but *sex is good*. Sexual intimacy in a covenant marriage according to God's design is a good thing, and something only a wife is permitted to provide her husband. She has the full power of doing good to him in this way through the vows of marriage and the blessing of the Father.

*"As we have opportunity, let us do good..."* Maybe you could plan some good with your husband this week, or even today.

# ❧Questions❧

Do you believe that sex is "doing good" to your spouse? How does your view of sex affect that belief?

_____

_____

_____

_____

_____

Have you used the opportunities you have to bless your husband with sexual intimacy? Where and how could you improve in this goal?

_____

_____

_____

_____

_____

## ❧*Prayer*❧

The Lord Our God is good. Dear Father, You have made sex to be a good thing, a blessing for my husband and me in marriage, a way to express and foster our intimacy. Please give me Your perspective of this act. Help me to find opportunities to do good to my husband in our marital bedroom. Give me a heart of generosity. In the name of my good Savior, Amen.

Week 30

## Are You Lovesick?

*Daughters of Jerusalem, I charge you— if you find my beloved,*
*what will you tell him? Tell him I am faint with love.*

— Song of Songs 5:8

F*aint with love"*—what an interesting phrase! The Hebrew word translated here as "faint" has been translated in various verses to mean weak, grieved, wounded, or sick. This wife in Song of Songs is saying she's lovesick for her husband.

She wants him. Bad. Can you relate?

In a majority of marriages, the husband has a stronger sexual desire than the wife, but one of the too-well-kept secrets is perhaps fifteen to twenty-five percent of marriages involve a wife with a higher drive than her husband. Some of these wives are sexually satisfied in their marriages, but some experience sexual rejection that wounds their hearts deeply. Then they have the added wound of feeling like oddballs, or freaks of nature.

For the wife in Song of Songs, this was a temporary circumstance. She desired her husband, looked for him, didn't find him, and felt lovesick. Many a Christian wife feels lovesick for her husband. And she wonders what's wrong with her and/or what's wrong with her husband that they don't fit the norm.

Many factors influence our sexual desire, but libido is a God-created aspect of our physiology and naturally varies from person to person. In every marriage, one spouse desires sex more than the other. Thus, it's perfectly normal and natural for the wife to be the one who gets a bit lovesick for her spouse.

## ❧*Questions*❧

Are you the higher-desire spouse in your marriage? If so, in what ways have you ever felt "*faint with love,*" or lovesick, for your husband?

_____

_____

_____

_____

_____

Have you intentionally or inadvertently downplayed the desire some Christian wives have for more sex in their marriage? Do you have any friends in your life who might feel lovesick for their husbands and need a word of encouragement?

_____

_____

_____

_____

_____

## ❧*Prayer*❧

Lord Jehovah, You created our bodies and infused them with a desire for physical intimacy. Then You provided marriage as the rightful place for that physical intimacy and blessed that covenant. But many marriages struggle with one spouse wanting more and one spouse wanting less. In my own marriage, we don't always see eye-to-eye on how often to have sex. Lord, help me to listen to my husband's desires, to recognize my own desires, and to seek unity regarding frequency of sexual intimacy. Give me compassion for those who struggle with desiring sexual connection more often than their spouse, and help me to speak encouragement to higher-desire wives who feel lovesick for their husbands. In the holy name of Your Son, Amen.

# Conception and Infertility

*So Boaz took Ruth and she became his wife.*
*When he made love to her, the Lord enabled her*
*to conceive, and she gave birth to a son.*

— RUTH 4:13

*But they were childless because Elizabeth was not*
*able to conceive, and they were both very old.*

— LUKE 1:7

Sexual intimacy has several functions in a marriage, but one of the most important for our families and society is reproduction. Most married couples desire that sex produce children at some point. For some, conception is a fairly easy accomplishment, but others walk a path of infertility, disappointment, and even despair.

When a couple yearns to be parents and that goal is fraught with obstacles or simply unachievable, sex itself can lose its meaning and its appeal. The marriage bed becomes a constant reminder of that desire too long withheld or the pressure to perform. The intimacy part of the sexual relationship can feel less important to either or both spouses than conceiving a child.

There is hope, however, in the stories of real people in the Bible who experienced both fertility and infertility. Take these couples as examples: Boaz and Ruth in the Old Testament, and Zechariah and Elizabeth in the New Testament. Both were godly couples who sought the Lord's will and both desired children, but one conceived quickly and the other experienced years of waiting, hoping, and hardship. Yet, both had good marriages. How do I know? You can read their stories and see the love and respect they afforded one another.

When a couple struggles to conceive, it requires intentional focus to remember that sex is not merely a means to an end. Even before the children arrive, you two are a family. You two are blessed. You two are fruitful in God's eyes. The fruit you bear is spiritual fruit to one another as you approach your marriage and the marriage bed with kindness, goodness, gentleness, and joy. Yes, it's important that marriages produce children, but more important that they produce love.

## ❧*Questions*❧

Have you and your husband ever experienced a time of infertility? How did that impact your view of the marriage bed?

_____

_____

_____

_____

_____

Do you know other couples who have struggled with infertility? Is there anyone going through this difficulty you can pray for, specifically for the health of their sexual intimacy?

_____

_____

_____

_____

_____

## ❧*Prayer*❧

Blessed Giver of Life, You know me completely—my hopes and my disappointments, my dreams and my despair. You see the pain of infertility in married couples everywhere, and You long to hold the hurting in Your loving arms. I pray, Lord, that the wounds of infertility will not rob the marriage bed of its beauty and its intimacy. Remind us that sex is more than a means to produce children, that You also use it to draw a couple closer together. Please bless these infertile couples with children, but regardless of the outcome, may we honor You with the fruit of the Spirit. In Jesus' name, Amen.

## Leave Your Life of Sin

*Jesus straightened up and asked her, "Woman, where are they? Has no one condemned you?"*

*"No one, sir," she said.*

*"Then neither do I condemn you," Jesus declared. "Go now and leave your life of sin."*

— JOHN 8:10-12[2]

---

[2]This passage is not in the earliest manuscripts. Yet, it is consistent with Jesus' approach and teaching and has been accepted as a true story nonetheless—perhaps passed around orally until finally written down. When and how it was added, we don't know. But I believe we can gain as Christians from its reading.

**R**eligious leaders brought a woman to Jesus for his judgment—a woman caught in adultery. Can you even imagine the horror of being caught in a sexually immoral moment, dragged by church leaders out into the streets (knowing the Law says the next step is stoning), and being presented before the holiest man alive, this man you've heard about named Jesus? Surely we've never experienced such trepidation and humiliation.

Yet many wives have experienced shame about their sexual behavior. They've felt the eyes of judgment upon them, labeling them as loose, broken, unworthy, sinful. If you made poor sexual decisions in your past, if you were tainted by your experiences and even written off by others, Jesus has words for you. He knows we all struggle with sin. He's not condemning you. He tells you to *"go and leave your life of sin"*—to discover instead a sexuality that honors Him, the intimacy of the marriage bed.

Have you forgiven yourself for past sins? Have you repented of immodesty, promiscuity, or adultery and accepted a newer, better understanding of God's design for sexual intimacy? Have you taken the fabric of your sexuality, yanked away the unraveled threads, and seen what a beautiful tapestry is left in your hands? *"Go and leave your life of sin."* Leave it completely behind and embrace the life of a new creature in Christ.

# ❧Questions❧

Do you, or your husband, have sexual sins from your past? How have these sins stuck with you and influenced your perspective of sex?

_____

_____

_____

_____

_____

Do you need to forgive yourself, or your husband, more fully? How does God see you, now that you've left your life of sin?

_____

_____

_____

_____

_____

## ❧*Prayer*❧

Holy Father, You believe the best of me, even in those times when I'm inclined to throw stones at myself. You have plans to prosper me and not to harm me, to give me hope and a future. Please help me to fully let go of my sinful past, to let go of my husband's sinful past, and to forgive those in my midst with a sexually sinful past—knowing we have left that life of sin. Guide me to a better understanding of sex as You intended, in the holy bonds of marriage, and help me to delight in that gift. In Jesus' name, Amen.

# Has He Wronged You?

*Make sure that nobody pays back wrong for wrong, but always try to be kind to each other and to everyone else.*

— 1 THESSALONIANS 5:15

**W**e know what the desire for retaliation feels like. We were wronged and seek justice, but somehow it morphs into a malicious desire to see the other hurt the way we hurt. It often happens in marriage, when our toes or our feelings get stepped on, and we pay back his wrong with our wrong.

The marriage bed is one of the places where we take retaliation. He doesn't complete the honey-do list? You deny him sex. He ignores your desire for attention? You deny him sex. He hurts your feelings? You deny him sex.

We tell ourselves it's simply that we don't feel like having sex, and there are times when that's true—when we are so deeply hurt or angry that connecting physically feels false and even painful. But how often do you really reach that point? How often instead are you paying back one wrong by committing another? By withholding sexual intimacy from your husband?

The Bible charges us to avoid this kind of behavior. 1 Corinthians 13:5 says that love keeps no records of wrongs. Instead, God commands us to *always try to be kind to each other.* If you feel wronged, deal with that issue. But don't withhold sexual intimacy to pay your husband back for a wrong he's committed. Ask yourself what kindness would look like for him. Consider that sex may foster deeper intimacy and understanding between you.

# ❧Questions❧

Think about the times you've felt wronged by your husband. Have you withheld physical intimacy to punish him?

_____

_____

_____

_____

_____

How can you move past feelings of hurt or anger and extend kindness to your husband? How would that impact your sexual intimacy and your marital relationship?

_____

_____

_____

_____

_____

## ❧*Prayer*❧

Dear God, I know that love involves kindness and forgiveness and perseverance. But sometimes I feel so hurt that I struggle to offer these to my husband. Shed Your light on those times when I am tempted to pay my husband back by withholding sexual intimacy. Lead me to a better path of offering kindness and grace, and give me the will and the wisdom to deal with our issues in a way that doesn't negatively impact our physical intimacy. In Jesus' name, Amen.

# Are You Under Attack?

*The thief comes only to steal and kill and destroy; I have come that they may have life, and have it to the full.*

— JOHN 10:10

**W**hat does Satan, the thief, want to steal, kill, and destroy about sex in your marriage? He likely desires to steal your joy, your right view of sex as God's creation, and your confidence in your body and desirability. He wants to kill your sexual desire, your opportunities to make love, and your connection to your husband. He longs to destroy your hope, your satisfaction, and your sense of intimacy.

Like a thief, you don't always know Satan's been there, attacking your marital bedroom. You may simply sense something is missing, gone, not as it should be. You wonder why you aren't experiencing what the Bible says is possible for your marriage bed. Where is that life *"to the full"* when it comes to sexual intimacy?

It may be that you and your husband are under attack—that you need to bond together and fight your mutual enemy.

Consider where the enemy has planted wrong messages about sex, where he has tried to convince you sex isn't or can't be good, where he has placed division between you and your husband. Jesus says He wants us to have a full life, and that includes God's provision for the marriage bed. How can you reclaim the rich, full sexual intimacy God wants you to have?

## ❧Questions❧

In what ways does Satan attack sexual intimacy in marriage? How has he been active within our culture and within your own marriage?

———————————————————————————

———————————————————————————

———————————————————————————

———————————————————————————

———————————————————————————

What feels like it's missing in your sexual intimacy with your husband? How can you mutually reclaim what the thief has tried to steal from your marriage bed?

———————————————————————————

———————————————————————————

———————————————————————————

———————————————————————————

———————————————————————————

## ❧*Prayer*❧

Loving Father, Your bounty extends even into our marriages and our sexual intimacy. Lord, how blessed we are to be Your children! Protect us from the enemy, who desires to steal, kill, and destroy the bonds of marriage in whatever way he can—including our marriage bed. Bring my husband and me together in unity to address those areas in which something is missing in our sex life. Help us to fight the enemy together, knowing You are the one who truly fights for us. Bless us with a full life lived according to Your will, including deep marital intimacy. In the name of Your Son, Amen.

# Sex and Love

*Do everything in love.*

— 1 CORINTHIANS 16:14

**W**e can spend a lot of time on scriptures that encourage word studies, historical background, context explanations, and thoughtful interpretation. This verse isn't one of them. It's straightforward and entirely understandable. Simple, really. "*Do everything in love.*"

But simple to understand isn't the same as simple to do. That single commandment to do *everything* in love won't be mastered by next Tuesday. It will take a lifetime of God renewing our minds and restoring our hearts and directing our steps to do *almost everything* in love. (Thanks to our Lord Jesus for His grace to cover the gaps.) Still, it's the target we must aim for every single day of our marriage—to do everything in love.

Do you carry that goal into your sexual life together? Do you act out of love as you choose when to engage, where to engage, how to engage, and why to engage? Do you allow love to infuse your level of desire, pleasure, and satisfaction with your marriage bed?

It's a tall order, but remember the Bible also says "*God is love*" (1 John 4:8). We can invite God into our choices, asking Him to help us approach our marital intimacy with love—so much love that *everything* we do sexually in our marriage connects us deeply to our husband and honors the Father.

# ❧*Questions*❧

Do you feel loved by your husband when you engage sexually? What would make you feel more loved?

_____

_____

_____

_____

_____

How can you connect your own decisions about when and how to engage sexually to your love for your husband? What would show love to him when it comes to sex?

_____

_____

_____

_____

_____

# ❧*Prayer*❧

Lord, Our Father, I often struggle with the commands that are simple to understand, because they are difficult to practice consistently. Lead me to a better understanding of how loving the sexual act is and can be between husband and wife. Whenever the subject of sex is raised in my marriage, recall these words to my mind: *"Do everything in love."* Guide me to make decisions that come from a place of love for my husband and for my God. In the name of Your Loving Son, Amen.

# What's Okay and What's Not

*Do not conform any longer to the pattern of this world, but be transformed by the renewing of your mind. Then you will be able to test and approve what God's will is—his good, pleasing and perfect will.*

— ROMANS 12:2

One of the most common questions asked by Christians about sex is what's okay and what's not—even in marriage. There's no straightforward, definitive list in the Bible of yeses and nos for the marital bedroom. Certainly there are sexual acts that honor God and others that don't comport with biblical principles of how we should treat one another. Some principles are obvious, such as avoiding anything adulterous, like including a third party in your marriage bed. But how can you discern what is holy and good for your marriage bed and what should be rejected?

Knowing God's will for any part of our life is about staying connected to Him and His Word. When it comes to sex in particular, it's easy to allow the *pattern of this world* to have a say, because the messages are so prevalent. What the secular world thinks about sex is proclaimed every time you turn on the radio or television, walk through a grocery store checkout or magazine stand, or even read the newspaper or online news. It takes intentional effort to renew your mind in Christ Jesus. We must saturate ourselves with God's Word, with godly counsel from fellow Christians, with the working of the Holy Spirit within us. We must meditate on His truths, His principles, His desire for our lives.

When you absorb a biblical perspective, it becomes far easier to tease out what's okay and what's not in the marriage bed. You begin asking yourself not merely, "Where in the Bible does it say I can't?" but rather, "Is this act in keeping with how God wants me to treat my spouse? Does this act benefit our relationship? Does it build up the body and the marriage God gave me?" You begin to test and approve God's *good, pleasing and perfect will.* Begin with the foundation of knowing Him, and you'll know better what He desires— even for your sexual intimacy.

# ❧Questions❧

Do you struggle knowing what's okay and what's not okay in the marriage bed? What specific acts have you wondered about?

_____

_____

_____

_____

_____

How can you determine what's okay? How can God's will for how we treat one another and biblical principles guide your decision-making?

_____

_____

_____

_____

_____

## *Prayer*

Dear God, I don't want to conform to the pattern of this world regarding sexuality. But it can be hard to know what's okay and what's not when it comes to sex. Draw me to Your Word and to a better understanding of the person You want me to become—even as my husband's lover. Help me to test and approve Your will for my life, including the marriage bed. Give me clarity and wisdom, so I can avoid ungodly practices but delight in the great sexual freedom You have given us. In Jesus' name, Amen.

# One

*This explains why a man leaves his father and mother and is joined to his wife, and the two are united into one.*

— Genesis 2:24 (NLT)

*Hear, O Israel: The Lord our God, the Lord is one.*

— Deuteronomy 6:4

**W**hat do these two passages have in common? In Hebrew, the word translated as "one"—referring to husband and wife and then to God—is the same: *echad*.

We worship a monotheistic God, a single entity who can be viewed as three persons as well. Which is a bit difficult to mentally grasp. But in marriage, we get a taste of this truth when two whole individuals join together in covenant marriage and sexual intimacy with one another.

Just as the Father, Son, and Holy Spirit are interconnected, interwoven, three persons in one, a husband and wife are connected with one another. Even in that moment of physical intimacy, it's clear that two distinct persons are joined together. They are two, yet one.

Sex isn't doing its job if you never feel that intense connection with your husband. Yes, there is a definite role in marriage for the quickie, the physical, even adventurous sex. However, God's ultimate plan is that we experience what He has—a sense of oneness with each other. If you haven't viewed marital sex that way, turn your mind to that picture. Sex should be intimate. Two become one.

## ❧Questions❧

What do you know about the relationship of God, Jesus, and the Holy Spirit? How is that like what God desires for marriages?

_____

_____

_____

_____

_____

Do you envision sex as a deeply intimate act? How can you foster that sense of oneness in the marriage bed?

_____

_____

_____

_____

_____

## ❧*Prayer*❧

The Lord my God, the Lord is One. Thank you, Father, for demonstrating oneness and intimacy through the Holy Trinity. Help me to better understand this mystery. Give me a desire for deep intimacy with my husband and an awareness of how sex contributes to our oneness. Help me to be naked before my husband, not just in my flesh, but in my being—so that our sexuality represents a deeper knowing of one another. Lord, give us "echad" in our marriage. In the name of Jesus and with the help of the Spirit I pray, Amen.

# For Your Own Good

*And now, Israel, what does the Lord your God ask of you but to fear the Lord your God, to walk in obedience to him, to love him, to serve the Lord your God with all your heart and with all your soul, and to observe the Lord's commands and decrees that I am giving you today for your own good?*

— DEUTERONOMY 10:12-13

Sex with only one person for the rest of your life is a hard sell. Plenty of people in the world are flabbergasted by this seemingly quaint notion from Christianity that you should only have sex with the person you marry. Moreover, they are at best skeptical and more likely mocking of the idea that married, religious people are having the best sex. But that's exactly what studies show.

Married couples with an active spiritual life and dedication to godly principles and praying together are "knocking boots" far more than the average. And why should that surprise us? God says it throughout the Bible, including this passage in which He assures us that His commands are not arbitrary and burdensome. Rather, He instructs us how to live so we can have the best life possible. Walking in obedience to His model for marriage and sex is for our own good. It produces the best harvest a person could reap.

If the world tries to convince you there's something better out there, if you read others' stories and wonder if maybe the grass is greener elsewhere, if you feel like being a godly girl won't give you the best sex...remember God's words. He wants the best for us, so He directs our path in the way that will lead to our health, happiness, and holiness. Believe in His promises: That if you walk in obedience, serve Him with all of yourself, and observe the Lord's commands, the outcome will be for your own good.

# ❧Questions❧

Do you feel like you're reaping the rewards of following God's plan for sexual intimacy yet? Why or why not?

_____

_____

_____

_____

_____

Why is God's design for sex within marriage superior? What good can it produce in our lives?

_____

_____

_____

_____

_____

## ❧*Prayer*❧

My Lord, my God, we are tempted to rebel against You at times, feeling that Your commands are difficult, burdensome, or hard to understand. But everything You command is for our own good. Help me to surrender entirely to Your design for sexual intimacy in my marriage, trusting the rewards will come. Turn my eyes and ears away from wrong messages and give me a heart of obedience, love, and service to You and all of Your Word. In Jesus' name, Amen.

## Inner Beauty

*Wives, in the same way submit yourselves to your own husbands so that, if any of them do not believe the word, they may be won over without words by the behavior of their wives, when they see the purity and reverence of your lives. Your beauty should not come from outward adornment, such as elaborate hairstyles and the wearing of gold jewelry or fine clothes. Rather, it should be that of your inner self, the unfading beauty of a gentle and quiet spirit, which is of great worth in God's sight.*

— 1 Peter 3:1-4

I don't think the apostle Peter was taught the "sandwich method" of presenting information. In the sandwich method, a person couches the meaty tough news in the middle—flanked by two fluffy pieces of bread encourage-ment. Such as, "I love that sweater [bread], but the scarf is the wrong color for you [meat]. How about trying the blue that brings out your eyes [bread]?" Instead, we were only six short words into the above verse when some of you wives read "submit" and thought, *Oh great, another submission verse.*

Yes, the verse starts with submission, but it's part of the whole concept of inner beauty. Maybe because Peter was a married man himself (Matthew 8:14), he understood the importance of a woman feeling beautiful. I don't know whether his wife was homely or drop-dead gorgeous, but he wanted a woman with "*unfading beauty.*"

So does your husband. We can spend a lot of time adorning ourselves with elaborate hairstyles, gold jewelry, fine clothes, or maybe even a handy pair of Spanx—all with the expectation that we will then feel beautiful. There's noth-ing wrong with enhancing your beauty a bit, but ultimately what makes you beautiful is that inner beauty. Men are attracted to wives who are easy and engaging to be around; who live out the godly principles of kindness, gentleness, joy, and encouragement; who attend to their spirit as well as their body. Are you the sort of woman your husband wants to be with? Wants to bed? Do you let your inner beauty show?

# ❧*Questions*❧

What makes you feel beautiful? What makes you feel *not* beautiful? How can you choose which messages to receive about your beauty?

_____

_____

_____

_____

_____

Think of someone you've known for a while who has become more physically appealing to you over time. What about their inner beauty showed through their exterior? What inner beauty do you have that you can show to your husband?

_____

_____

_____

_____

_____

## ❧*Prayer*❧

Heavenly Father, You have made me beautiful. But my spirit and my actions can lessen or increase my appeal to others, including my husband. Please give me a submissive, pure, reverent, gentle, quiet spirit. Help me to welcome my husband with my words and my behaviors so he will be drawn to me and my beauty. Let me see myself from Your perspective, as a beautiful daughter of the King. Make me beautiful inside. In my Savior's name, Amen.

# Modesty

*The Lord says,*
*"The women of Zion are haughty,*
*walking along with outstretched necks,*
*flirting with their eyes,*
*strutting along with swaying hips,*
*with ornaments jingling on their ankles.*

*Therefore the Lord will bring sores on the*
*heads of the women of Zion;*
*the Lord will make their scalps bald."*

— ISAIAH 3:16-17

**O**uch. Bald and sore-ridden scalps? What a tough judgment against those immodest and flirtatious women! While I doubt God is planning to yank the hairs from our heads today—or let's face it, there would be a lot of bald pop singers—the underlying principle remains the same. God does not want His daughters displaying themselves like prize beef cattle at a meat market. Instead, we are His treasured possession (Deuteronomy 7:6).

We must distinguish between being free and generous with our bodies in the marital bedroom and maintaining modesty and propriety out in the world. Your husband should know how sexy you are; your co-worker should not. Sometimes we get those things mixed up. Indeed, some wives withhold sexually from their husbands while dressing suggestively and flirting openly with men outside the home. Perhaps a wife rationalizes getting attention from other males because she feels neglected in some way by her own husband. However, read that verse again, and tell me if you really want to go down that path.

The Bible paints a picture of a husband and wife who should be comfortable and confident sharing their bodies with one another (see 1 Corinthians 7:3-5; Song of Songs). They should desire and delight in one another. However, the Word is also imminently clear that modesty and propriety are how we should approach the outer world.

So flirt with your eyes. Sway your hips. Go ahead. But do it all for your *husband*. That's where sexy belongs.

## ❧*Questions*❧

Define modesty for yourself. What do you believe are appropriate guidelines?

_____

_____

_____

_____

_____

How should your attitude toward sexual behavior change when it comes to your husband? What "privileges" should he receive as your partner in covenant marriage?

_____

_____

_____

_____

_____

# *Prayer*

Jehovah God, You are loving and faithful and patient with Your people. You are a God of unimaginable love. But I also know You are willing to bring wrath upon Your people to awaken them from sin, as you did in the days of Isaiah. Show me any unacceptable behaviors in my own life that resemble those of these haughty women and give me Your heart regarding modesty and propriety in the world. Help me to make the distinction when it comes to my marriage bed, allowing me to be free, flirtatious, and generous with my body to my husband. Give me wisdom to discern. In His holy name, Amen.

## More Generosity

*Give and it will be given to you. A good measure, pressed down, shaken together, and running over, will be poured into your lap. For with the measure you use, it will be measured to you.*

— LUKE 6:38

**H**ow giving are you in the marital bedroom? Would your husband need a teaspoon or a gallon container to measure your generosity?

If God hasn't blessed your marriage's sexual intimacy, consider whether you might be holding something back from your husband. Of course, problems aren't always the result of one person not giving enough, but not having an open heart and an open hand toward your spouse will cause problems. We're called to go above and beyond in the giving department, pouring out to our husband the way God has poured into us.

What more can you give? Is it more frequent sex? Is it more affection? Is it open communication? Is it reassurance? Start pouring it out, watching it overflow past the rim and spill into the other areas of your marriage and your life. Give as God gives to you.

# ❧*Questions*❧

Would your husband describe you as generous regarding marital intimacy? Why or why not?

_____

_____

_____

_____

_____

In what way are you holding back something from your husband in the marriage bed? Do you have a biblical reason for holding it back, or do you need to open yourself up to more generosity?

_____

_____

_____

_____

_____

## ❧*Prayer*❧

Lord, You are the giver of all good things. I long for Your blessings in my marriage and in my life. Help me to see where I have been stingy with my love in the sexual realm and to open myself up to generosity. If my husband has been stingy in some ways to me, help me to forgive him, to do my part in giving, and to communicate how we can come together and be united in pursuing the sexual intimacy You intended for us. May I bless my husband continually, and bless me according to my actions and Your overwhelming grace. In Jesus' name, Amen.

# Sexual Sin

*My eyes are on all their ways; they are not hidden
from me, nor is their sin concealed from my eyes.*

— JEREMIAH 16:17

Sexual sins are often easier to hide than other offenses. Excluding attention-grabbing celebrities, sexual sins tend to happen in secret—with two people, or even a single person. Those engaged in sexual immorality hide behind closed doors, delete Internet histories, keep secrets to themselves, rationalize their wrongdoing. We can fool ourselves into believing our private actions are protected against revelation and scrutiny.

Yet, God knows what we do in our private spaces. If you or your husband is steeped in sexual sin, you're not really getting away with it. Even if no one else in the world is making you accountable, God is fully aware of what's going on.

He's not hovering up there waiting to zap you for any infraction, but He does know our heart, our attitudes, our actions, our excuses. He longs for sinners to come into the light and let Him purge their lives of evil (1 John 1:6-7). We can rest assured that God knows.

If you're engaged in sexual sin, come into the light. Your sin isn't concealed anyway. And if your husband is involved in sexual sin, know that God is aware. He sees and knows and aches for you. He wants your whole marriage in the light as well.

# ❧Questions❧

Are you dealing with personal sexual sin? If so, what? If your husband is involved in sexual sin, what is he doing (that he may even believe he's concealing from others)?

_____

_____

_____

_____

_____

How does your understanding that *God knows* affect your approach to the problem? Do you take comfort in knowing a compassionate God knows exactly what's going on?

_____

_____

_____

_____

_____

## ❧*Prayer*❧

Our Heavenly Father, You are omniscient, knowing everything that happens on earth and in our hearts. You see deeply into our minds and our souls. You comfort us in our trouble and rebuke us in our sin. Lord, help me to lay everything bare before you and to bring my temptations and my wrongdoing to Your throne—asking forgiveness and guidance to avoid sexual sin. I pray my husband will be open and honest with me and with You, Lord, as well. Shine light on any secret sins and lead us to the deeper intimacy You desire us to have. In the name of Jesus, Amen.

# A Quarrelsome Wife

*Better to live on a corner of the roof than
share a house with a quarrelsome wife.*

— PROVERBS 21:9

This verse is only one of several proverbs warning men about the hardship of having a *"quarrelsome wife."* This circumstance is so distasteful to a husband, he'd rather leave the warm comfort of his bed and sleep on the roof.

Do you know what doesn't happen sleeping alone on a roof? Sex.

What you do outside the bedroom impacts what happens inside the bedroom. Are you quarrelsome? A nag? Hard to live with? Is it therefore hard for your husband to want to be close? Or is he physically close only long enough to meet a sexual need, but not drawing close emotionally and spiritually to you in the marriage bed?

What can you do as a wife to be more appealing and inviting? What godly virtues can replace that quarrelsome bent?

## ❧*Questions*❧

When have you been quarrelsome with your husband? How does he react to nagging and argumentativeness?

_____

_____

_____

_____

_____

Do you and your husband need to address and resolve certain issues to relieve relationship tension? Can you let some things go? What would help you to be less quarrelsome or feel less resentful? (Concentrate on choices you have control over.)

_____

_____

_____

_____

_____

## ❧*Prayer*❧

Dear Lord, at times I have been quarrelsome—either outright with my words and behavior or holding on to a bitter attitude. Refocus my heart on loving my husband, forgiving him of slights, giving him grace, and pursuing peace. Measure my words and tame my tongue and my thoughts. Let my demeanor be appealing and inviting, displaying my inner beauty so that my husband will fully desire me. In the name of my Redeemer, Amen.

# The Comfort of Sex

*Then David comforted his wife Bathsheba, and he went to her and made love to her. She gave birth to a son, and they named him Solomon. The Lord loved him.*

— I SAMUEL 12:24

**B**athsheba was grieving the death of her newborn child, a heart-rending experience for any mother. In the face of this crisis, we might expect a scripture like, "Then David comforted his wife Bathsheba; he listened to her talk through her pain all night long," or "Then David comforted his wife Bathsheba; he held her close and let her cry in his arms." Instead, the verse is *"Then David comforted his wife Bathsheba, and he went to her and made love to her."* Can sex itself be comforting?

Sexual intimacy can comfort in times of anxiety or grief. Sex releases physical tension built up inside, through a wash of certain brain chemicals such as oxytocin and serotonin, which provide a sense of calm and well-being. Sex also reassures you of your husband's presence and constant love, giving you an anchor to hold onto in a raging storm. And that intimacy can transport you, even for a moment, beyond the current struggles in your life. Making love can take you away from the worries and hurt of your current circumstances to a place of pleasure and joy.

Among the many benefits of God's gift of sexual intimacy in marriage is this sense of comfort we can feel. It can provide a buffer against the storms of life and soothe the pain we sometimes experience. Like David to Bathsheba, your husband's lovemaking can be a source of comfort.

## ❧Questions❧

Have you ever made love during a time of crisis or grief? How did that experience impact you?

_____

_____

_____

_____

_____

How can making love comfort your husband? What benefits can you see to reaching out for one another sexually when life hands you difficulties?

_____

_____

_____

_____

_____

## ❧*Prayer*❧

Lord, You've not promised our lives will be pain-free in this world, but You have promised to walk with us through difficulties. Thank You for the gift of a mate to walk with me as well. Help me to reach for my husband when life is tough and not push him away. I pray that I can prioritize our love-making even in times of crisis and grief and that I can find comfort in our marriage bed. Help me to also comfort my husband when he goes through struggles, by physically reassuring him of our love. In the name of Jesus, Amen.

# Enthralled by Beauty

*Listen, daughter, and pay careful attention:*
*Forget your people and your father's house.*

*Let the king be enthralled by your beauty;*
*honor him, for he is your lord.*

*The city of Tyre will come with a gift,*
*people of wealth will seek your favor.*

*All glorious is the princess within her chamber;*
*her gown is interwoven with gold.*

*In embroidered garments she is led to the king;*
*her virgin companions follow her—*
*those brought to be with her.*

*Led in with joy and gladness,*
*they enter the palace of the king.*

— PSALM 45:10-15

Among the psalms praising God is this royal wedding song written by the sons of Korah. The first part of the psalm is directed toward the king, but this second section addresses the king's bride. While you may not relate to reveling in all that pomp and circumstance and entering a palace right after your *I do's*, one sentiment here still informs our marriages: "*Let the king be enthralled by your beauty.*"

Easier said than done, at times.

Most men are highly visually stimulated, created that way by our Heavenly Father. When you fell in love and decided to marry, something about your appearance, your body, your beauty attracted your husband. That beauty remains appealing, and he wants to *see it*.

Do you hide in the closet to dress? Turn off the lights to make love? Become overly self-conscious when he stares longingly at your body? The Bible doesn't say that we must be perfect to draw the eyes of our beloved, but we are told to let him look. Allow your husband to be enthralled by you! By how God created you female, with a more fragile form and tender flesh and feminine curves. Welcome your husband's gaze by offering him the time he desires to simply look at you and be enthralled.

# ❧Questions❧

What makes your feminine form interesting to your husband? What about your body might enthrall him?

_____

_____

_____

_____

_____

Are you comfortable letting your husband look at you? Dressed? Naked? How can you encourage and welcome his gaze?

_____

_____

_____

_____

_____

## ❧*Prayer*❧

Dear King of Kings, thank You for the beautiful body You gave me. Help me to appreciate what about my beauty appeals to my husband and to allow him to gaze at me lovingly. Increase my comfort and confidence, so I can remove my clothes and feel relaxed and cherished in his presence. Let my husband see me as Your handiwork and be enthralled. In the name of Jesus, Amen.

# Your Thoughts about Sex

*Finally, brothers and sisters, whatever is true, whatever is noble, whatever is right, whatever is pure, whatever is lovely, whatever is admirable—if anything is excellent or praiseworthy—think about such things. Whatever you have learned or received or heard from me, or seen in me—put it into practice. And the God of peace will be with you.*

— Philippians 4:8-9

**W**hat are your thoughts regarding sexual intimacy? Do they reflect the things that are true, noble, right, pure, lovely, and admirable about God's creation of sex?

The world desires to turn our hearts and minds from those things that are excellent and praiseworthy about the sexual act between husband and wife, making sex instead a jumble of selfish and perverse thoughts. Or maybe simply physical thoughts about pleasure, prowess, and peaks. But when God creates something, it is true, noble, right, pure, lovely, admirable.

Do you envision sex that way? Do you accept it as a good, righteous, and beautiful gift from our Father?

Practice turning your thoughts to what is best about your sexual relationship with your husband. Shove out anything that keeps you from viewing sex as a deep, meaningful, God-honoring act in a covenant marriage. If your own sex life isn't quite there, keep your thoughts on what God intended sexual intimacy to be, and your own view may be the starting point for positive change in your marriage.

## ❧*Questions*❧

Considering these attributes—true, noble, right, pure, lovely, admirable—which one or ones do you struggle to see in your sexual intimacy? Why?

_____

_____

_____

_____

_____

What is excellent and praiseworthy about God's design for sexual intimacy in marriage?

_____

_____

_____

_____

_____

## ❧*Prayer*❧

God, Your creation is true, noble, right, pure, lovely, and admirable. Everything that comes from Your hands is worthy of praise. Sometimes, however, we forget that sexual intimacy in marriage is among Your noble and admirable gifts. Turn my mind to focus on these aspects of sex in my marriage. Help me to see how You have blessed this act with goodness and beauty. When my mind strays from viewing sex with my husband positively, refocus my thoughts on Your perspective of this gift to married couples. Thank You, Lord, for Your excellent and praiseworthy gift of sex to my marriage. In Jesus' name, Amen.

# Redemption

*Then Joshua son of Nun secretly sent two spies from Shittim.
"Go, look over the land," he said, "especially Jericho." So
they went and entered the house of a prostitute named
Rahab and stayed there. The king of Jericho was told, "Look,
some of the Israelites have come here tonight to spy out the
land." So the king of Jericho sent this message to Rahab:
"Bring out the men who came to you and entered your
house, because they have come to spy out the whole land."*

*But the woman had taken the two men and hidden them.
She said, "Yes, the men came to me, but I did not know
where they had come from. At dusk, when it was time to
close the city gate, they left. I don't know which way they
went. Go after them quickly. You may catch up with them."
(But she had taken them up to the roof and hidden them
under the stalks of flax she had laid out on the roof.)*

— JOSHUA 2:1-6

*But Joshua spared Rahab the prostitute, with her family and all
who belonged to her, because she hid the men Joshua had sent as
spies to Jericho—and she lives among the Israelites to this day.*

— JOSHUA 6:25

Ensconced in the story of the Israelites conquering the mighty city of Jericho is this story of one pivotal woman, Rahab. Mind you, she was a foreigner in a pagan land, a prostitute, and technically an enemy. She should have gone down with the crumbling walls of Jericho, but instead she kept two Israelite spies safe, acknowledged God (v. 8-11), and requested the Israelites rescue her family from certain destruction (v. 12-13).

After Rahab and her family were spared, she could have gone anywhere. Surely, there was another town where she could make a living as a prostitute. But she moved in with God's people. She lived among them. And not only that, the next time we see her in the Bible, she's listed in Jesus' bloodline (Matthew 1:5).

So what does this story have to do with sex and marriage?

Rahab could have allowed guilt to weigh her down and labeled herself a whore for the rest of her life. But she adopted a new identity with God's people. We needn't hang on to labels from our past. Whether your past involves promiscuity (like Rahab), sexual abuse, or even sexual misunderstandings in your own marriage, it isn't destiny. It's the *past*. If Rahab can overcome her sexual past and leave this legacy, how can we limit ourselves? And God?

You can forge a better, godly future with a beautiful legacy of love and sex, *God's way*. Whenever you doubt being able to move beyond a problematic past, remember Rahab, the great-great-great...grandma of our Lord Jesus. And remember how God redeemed her.

# ❧*Questions*❧

What negative sexual experiences linger from your past?

_____

_____

_____

_____

_____

Describe the sexual intimacy you want to have (or want to want) with your husband. What legacy of intimacy would you like to foster for your marriage?

_____

_____

_____

_____

_____

## ❧*Prayer*❧

Lord, You have redeemed us—each one of us—regardless of what difficult past we came from. Create in me a true understanding of Your redemption, even in the area of sexual intimacy. Help me to move beyond any negative experiences or messages or misunderstandings from my past and into Your holy design for marital intimacy with my husband. Whenever I feel change is impossible, remind me of Rahab and so many others You rescued and redeemed. Help me to create a positive legacy for my family and my future through a healthy marriage and a holy marriage bed. In the name of our true Redeemer, Amen.

# Aligning Your Desires

*Take delight in the Lord, and he will give
you the desires of your heart.*

— Psalm 37:4

All too often, we focus on the latter half of that equation. We want God to give us the desires of our heart. When it comes to sexual intimacy, maybe you desire your husband would stop asking you for sex so much. Maybe you wish he'd want sex more often. Maybe you desire that he romance you more or help out with the household chores more, and then you'd be more willing. Maybe you want him to do something different in the bedroom or in the way he initiates sex.

We each have desires in our heart surrounding sexual intimacy in our marriage. There are things we want. But this verse says we must begin by taking delight in the Lord. God doesn't promise to give us the desires of our heart unless we first align our desires with His. We need to pause and ponder what it looks like to take delight in the Lord. How about when it comes to our marital intimacy?

God wants us to have the same kind of unselfish, loving, unity-seeking approach He takes toward us. He wants us to see sex the way He created it and to delight in His design. We may need to spend more time asking ourselves where our desires have gotten out of whack with what God wants for our marriage bed and then put them back on track with God's perspective.

We must first take delight in God's design, in God's heart for our marriage, in God Himself—the Creator of intimacy. Then we can make our requests of God, knowing our desires are in sync with our Father.

# ❧Questions❧

What are the *"desires of your heart"* when it comes to sexual intimacy in your marriage? What do you wish was different between you and your husband?

_____

_____

_____

_____

_____

Be honest: Are any of your desires selfish or divisive or unloving toward your husband? How can you realign your desires with those of God and take delight in Him?

_____

_____

_____

_____

_____

## ❧*Prayer*❧

Father God, You know the desires of my heart. Some of my desires are pure and good and in line with what You want for me and my life, but others are selfish and steeped in fear or misunderstanding or anger or hurt. Please sweep away my selfish desires and replace them with what You yearn for my marriage to be. Lord, I delight in You! I delight in Your design for covenant marriage and for sexual intimacy. Give me Your mind and Your heart and Your desires when it comes to my marriage and my marriage bed. In the name of our Savior and Lord, Amen.

## An Inconvenience

*I slept but my heart was awake.*

*Listen! My beloved is knocking:*
*"Open to me, my sister, my darling,*
*my dove, my flawless one.*

*My head is drenched with dew,*
*my hair with the dampness of the night."*

*I have taken off my robe —*
*must I put it on again?*

*I have washed my feet —*
*must I soil them again?*

— SONG OF SONGS 5:2-3

The most revealing two words in this passage are "*must I?*" This woman's husband had likely been on a trip, came home in the middle of the night, and wanted to immediately be close and intimate with his wife. But she was exhausted and didn't want to get out of bed, put on her robe, soil her feet on the dusty floor, and open the door for him.

Like the wife in Song of Songs, sometimes we take this same attitude when hubby suggests sex. He makes an advance, and we think, "Seriously? Now? But I'm ____!" Fill in the blank with sleeping, doing laundry, watching a TV show, etc.

Sex can feel like a lot of trouble. It requires us to shift our mental focus, to be awake and engaged, to bare our bodies when we may not feel like it, to "soil the sheets" (meaning more laundry this week), to set aside a chunk of time and attention to be physical with your husband. We can end up with the question running through our heads or even out of our mouths: *Must I?*

The answer to that question is *It depends*. Do you want to have a quality, long-lasting, intimate marriage? If your answer to that question is yes, then you'll need to get over the reluctance hump at times. You needn't have sex at the snap of his fingers; you're not his beck-and-call girl. However, if your husband is inviting you into sexual intimacy, it's important to him, and you shouldn't turn down his advances simply because it's inconvenient. Relationships are always inconvenient in some respect, but they are also fulfilling when we invest in them with our whole heart and selves.

*Must I?* is the wrong question. Instead, the question should be *Why not?* Why not go out of your way to be one-flesh with your husband in the marriage bed? If he's knocking, why not open that door?

# ❧Questions❧

What feels inconvenient or too-much-trouble when it comes to having sex? How can you address those issues?

_____

_____

_____

_____

_____

What can you do to make sex a routine and convenient event for both of you?

_____

_____

_____

_____

## ❧*Prayer*❧

Holy Father, You have shown what it is to be inconvenienced for those You love. Again and again, You go out of Your way to care for Your children, and I thank You for Your love and example. Help me to go out of my way to be sexually intimate with my husband. Let the question in my head never be "must I?" but rather "Why not?" Fill my heart with Your love and my mind with Your perspective of my husband and my marriage bed. Make me a willing and eager participant in our sexual intimacy. In Jesus' name, Amen.

## Building Him Up

*Do not let any unwholesome talk come out of your mouths,
but only what is helpful for building others up according to their needs, that it may benefit those who listen.*

— EPHESIANS 4:29

**W**ords matter. It's astounding how many Bible verses address our need to pay attention to our speech and how it impacts others. This verse challenges us to be helpful, building up, beneficial to those who listen to our words.

In the marriage bed, the one listening is your husband. So how do your words meet this challenge? Are you encouraging, loving, complimentary to him when he tries to initiate or when you make love? Oftentimes, we wives don't carefully consider the impact our words about sex have on our husband. But we can tear him down or build him up with what we say.

More specifically, the Bible says that our words should build others up *"according to their needs."* Not according to what we feel or how tired we are or how nervous we may be. Instead, our barometer for how we're doing with our words in the marital bedroom is whether they build up our husband according to what he needs. Consider those needs, and consider your words. Make your marriage bed a place where he feels built up and benefited.

# ❧*Questions*❧

What has your speech communicated to your husband about sexual intimacy in your marriage? Have your words reflected the message you want to send?

_____

_____

_____

_____

_____

What does your husband need to hear? What words would benefit him most?

_____

_____

_____

_____

_____

## *Prayer*

Holy God, I thank you for the gift of language—for the ability to communicate what we feel and know with words. Help me to use my words to build others up and benefit them according to their needs. Give me insight on how to best do this for my husband and my marriage bed. Embolden me to tell him what a great lover he is and how much I appreciate his lovemaking. Rid me of any unwholesome talk about Your gift of sexual intimacy and replace it with words that will benefit my husband and build him up. In the name of my precious Savior, Amen.

# Teaching Others

*Likewise, teach the older women to be reverent in the way they live, not to be slanderers or addicted to much wine, but to teach what is good. Then they can urge the younger women to love their husbands and children, to be self-controlled and pure, to be busy at home, to be kind, and to be subject to their husbands, so that no one will malign the word of God.*

— TITUS 2:3-5

**T**his passage may seem a bit antiquated to today's woman, as if older women are merely instructing younger women to be productive, domestic, docile wives. We might even conjure up images of a 1950s housewife consumed with putting dinner on the table and bringing a drink to her hard-working hubby when he walks through the door, all the while ignoring her own needs. Well, get beyond your presumptions, because the Bible has truth to speak here, even if First Century culture was different from today.

In this chapter, the apostle Paul gives his younger partner in ministry, Titus, some parameters on what to teach families. How to Be a Good Wife 101 is supposed to be taught by wives who've already been through the graduate school of a long, healthy marriage. And the lessons aren't supposed to be about not burning the casserole or things to do with bored children on a rainy day (not that I don't need those lessons). The priority is teaching principles: self-control, purity, productivity, kindness, and service to your husband. Why? So that no one will discount God on account of someone's bad marriage.

What about these principles in the marital bedroom? Shouldn't older Christian wives teach younger Christian wives how to display godly principles when it comes to sex in marriage? Shouldn't we be concerned that we have healthy sex lives in our marriages, so that no one (including ourselves) can malign the Word of God because of a bad marriage?

It's biblical for us to encourage happy marriages, holy wives, and healthy sexuality to honor our Father and strengthen our message to the world. Godly sexual intimacy should become a respectful part of our conversation in Christian women's circles, Bible studies, ladies' retreats, devotionals, and mentoring. Older women—the ones who've figured some things out—should teach the younger women. And all of our marriages will be strengthened.

# ❧*Questions*❧

How does your church do when it comes to addressing the topic of sexual intimacy in marriage? Is it a welcomed or a taboo subject? Why?

_____

_____

_____

_____

_____

Have you received godly teaching about sex in marriage from a more mature Christian wife? Have you given such teaching to another wife? What can you personally do to encourage quality mentoring for yourself or to others?

_____

_____

_____

_____

_____

## ❦*Prayer*❦

Holy Father, Your Word encourages us to teach one another what we've learned. Thank you for your beautiful plan for the Church and the fellowship of other Christians to bolster our walk of faith. Please help me speak with boldness and encouragement to younger wives in my midst about biblical sexuality in marriage. When I have struggles myself, place before me a female mentor who will share godly wisdom. Empower my church to address this topic respectfully and effectively so we can strengthen all of our marriages and increase our outreach to others. In the name of Jesus, Amen.

# What the Word Says

*Do not merely listen to the word, and so deceive your-
selves. Do what it says. Anyone who listens to the word but
does not do what it says is like someone who looks at his
face in a mirror and, after looking at himself, goes away
and immediately forgets what he looks like. But whoever
looks intently into the perfect law that gives freedom, and
continues in it—not forgetting what they have heard,
but doing it—they will be blessed in what they do.*

— JAMES 1:22-25

Of course, following God's design for sexual intimacy begins with knowing what it is. As with any other aspect of the Christian life, we begin by hearing from God Himself—listening to His Word. But it doesn't end there. Knowing what we should do doesn't mean we do it. It requires intentionality, commitment, and perseverance to continue in "*the perfect law that gives freedom*" and experience God's full blessing.

It's easy to forget how important God's gift of sexual intimacy is to our marriage when we're faced with daily demands on our time, relational challenges, discomfort and discouragement with our bodies, physical or physiological obstacles, and more. We can rationalize our decisions to stray from God's Word when it comes to being the kind of wife we should be in the marriage bed. We *listen* to the Word, but we forget what that healthy sexual wife looks like in the mirror. We walk away and give it little or no further thought.

"*Do what it says.*" Perhaps that's the most straightforward statement in the New Testament: Do what the Word says. So the Word says to share your body freely with your husband (1 Corinthians 7:3-5)? So the Word says to keep the marriage bed pure (Hebrews 13:4)? So the Word says to flee from sexual immorality (1 Corinthians 6:18)? So the Word says to drink your fill of love in the marriage bed (Song of Songs 5:1)? *Do what it says.*

Whatever you learn about God's plan for sexual intimacy, carry it out. Then see what blessings your faithful obedience brings to you and/or your marriage.

## ❧Questions❧

Do you feel you understand God's design for sexual intimacy in marriage? Do you need to spend more time in the Word to discern His plan?

_____

_____

_____

_____

_____

What commands or examples for sexual intimacy from the Bible are especially hard for you to carry out? Where do you struggle to follow God's Word in this area?

_____

_____

_____

_____

_____

## ❧*Prayer*❧

Holy God, thank You for Your Word—for sharing with us Your perfect plan for marriage and sexual intimacy. Give me a hunger to know and absorb what You desire for my marriage and my marriage bed. Open my eyes and my heart as I read scriptures that shed light on the intimacy a husband and wife should have in Christ Jesus. Help me to hold Your Word in my heart and do what it says. Even when the blessings are not immediate, help me to continue in obedience and hope—knowing You are faithful to Your promises. In Christ Jesus, Amen.

# Acknowledgments

**My Heavenly Father**—who has blessed me in more ways than I thought possible. Lord, thank You for Your ongoing grace in my life. I don't deserve all I've received from Your generous hand. Thank You especially for Your Word. Without it, I would never have the holy and happy marriage I've come to enjoy.

**My husband**—whom my blog fans know as "Spock" (my nickname for Mr. Logical Hubby). May we have many more years to boldly go through this life together. I'll love you forever and a day.

**My sons**—who are, thankfully, more supportive of me ministering to marriages than embarrassed that their mom writes about sex. I pray God will someday bless you with amazing marriages and a lifetime of intimacy with the one you love. (Oh, and when that happens, I want grandkids. Just sayin'.)

**My readers at** *Hot, Holy & Humorous*—who inspire and encourage me to keep writing. Thanks for being strong supporters of marriage and my partners in the gospel! (See Philippians 1:4-6.)

# Author's Note

If you enjoyed this book, please consider leaving a review and recommending it to friends.

You might also enjoy the following by J. Parker:

### Hot, Holy & Humorous

Do you want to be a hottie in the bedroom without sacrificing holiness? How can you make the most of God's gift of sexual intimacy in marriage?

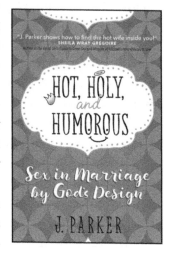

Wrongful thinking and behaviors regarding sex permeate our culture. Christians need to reclaim sexuality and enjoy it in the way God intended.

God does not shy away from the subject of sex. The Bible shows a better way in every area—including the marital bedroom.

In *Hot, Holy, and Humorous*, author J. Parker gives candid advice for wives from a foundation of faith with a splash of humor.

This book can boost your sex savvy and improve your marital intimacy. And guess what? With God's perfect design, you and your spouse can enjoy the most amazing sex!

# *About the Author*

J. Parker writes at *Hot, Holy & Humorous*, where she uses a biblical perspective and a blunt sense of humor to foster Christian sexuality in marriage.

When she isn't writing about godly sex or doing "research" with her husband, J writes fiction; hugs, disciplines, or cracks jokes with her kids (whichever is needed in the moment); and daydreams about having a personal chef and an on-call massage therapist.

Check out J's blog at www.hotholyhumorous.com or follow her on Twitter at @hotholyhumorous, Facebook at HotHolyHumorous, or Pinterest at hotholyhumorous.

Made in the USA
Las Vegas, NV
21 August 2022